HOUSE, DON'T FALL ON ME

MAIDHC DAINÍN Ó SÉ

HOUSE, DON'T FALL ON ME

MAIDHC DAINÍN Ó SÉ

Translated by Gabriel Fitzmaurice

MERCIER PRESS

WHAT YOU NEED TO READ

MERCIER PRESS
Douglas Village, Cork
www.mercierpress.ie

Trade enquiries to Columba Mercier Distribution,
55a Spruce Avenue, Stillorgan Industrial Park, Blackrock, Dublin

First published in 1987 by Coiscéim

978 1 85635 550 6

10 9 8 7 6 5 4 3 2 1

*This publication has received support from the Heritage Council under the 2007
Publications Grant Scheme*

AN
CHOMHAIRLE
OIDHREACHTA

THE
HERITAGE
COUNCIL

Mercier Press receives financial assistance from
the Arts Council/An Chomhairle Ealaíon

Printed and bound by J.H. Haynes & Co. Ltd, Sparkford

Translator's Note

Why this translation? I first read *A Thig Ná Tit Orm* about twenty years ago when I reviewed it for Raidió Na Gaeltachta. I loved it. I knew its author, Maidhc Dainín Ó Sé (for the purposes of this translation 'Mike Daneen O'Shea'). I had played music and sung with him in his native Corca Dhuibhne and at Writers' Week in Listowel. I understood what he was about.

In June 2006, my son John sat his Leaving Certificate examination. One of the books he was required to study was *A Thig Ná Tit Orm*. He loved it. He suggested to me that I translate it. I didn't need a second prompting.

I rang Maidhc Dainín and asked his permission to translate his book. His reply was: 'A Chríost, cuir Béarla maith air' ('Christ, put good English on it'). Assuming that what he meant was to render it into standard English (whatever that is), that is the one thing I couldn't do. His Irish is colloquial, conversational and without any airs and graces. Reading his book again, what struck me was how close in tone and syntax, rhythm and vocabulary, his Irish is to the dialect (of English) we spoke in north Kerry up to the 1950s. If my mother taught me 'good English' at home, I was smart enough to use the local dialect out on the street. This dialect has now all but disappeared.

This is the dialect I have chosen for this translation. Grammatically and syntactically it seems to be all over the place. But in its rhythm, inversions and localisms it is as close to Maidhc Dainín's Irish as the English language can get. I haven't used the north Kerry dialect in its unlettered purity. Like George

Fitzmaurice, especially, and writers like Bryan MacMahon and John B. Keane, I have sought to make a literary language of it. George Fitzmaurice, writing in the early 1900s, used it to brilliant effect. He employed transliterations from the Irish (for instance 'pusheen' for puisín (a kitten), 'high-fiddle' for aghaidh-fidil (a mask), and so on – words I grew up with in Moyvane in the early 1950s). Except where absolutely necessary, for instance where there is no suitable English equivalent, I have chosen to translate such words, not transliterate. A certain flavour is lost in this process, but a twenty-first century audience, I feel, would require such a translation.

So. It has been a joy to encounter Maidhc Dainín's Irish again. His book has been described as a cross between *Jimín Mháire Thaidhg* and *Dialann Deoraí*, and I wouldn't disagree with that. He has a story to tell, a lively, fast-paced account of growing up in the west Kerry Gaeltacht in the 1940s, emigration, first to England and later to the United States, and his eventual return home.

It is a joy to read. It was also a joy to translate – to put myself in touch with a dialect of English that is as close as that language can get to the Irish language, to feel and breathe and write in a space between languages, to recreate one language in terms of another.

Mark Twain, in his 'Explanatory' note to *Huckleberry Finn*, says of the dialects he used in his book: 'The shadings have not been done in a haphazard fashion, or by guesswork; but painstakingly, and with the trustworthy guidance and support of personal familiarity.' Likewise with this translation.

I want to thank Maidhc Dainín Ó Sé for his advice, suggestions, corrections (both to my text and to his original book which contains a few minor inaccuracies) and his wholehearted support and encouragement as I undertook the delightful task of translating *A Thig Ná Tit Orm*. I leave it to the reader to decide if I have succeeded. Here is Maidhc Dainín Ó Sé's *House, Don't Fall On Me!*

Enjoy!

Gabriel Fitzmaurice

1

The first Monday of September, 1947. My mother put me in a clean trousers and shirt. She washed my face with a rough towel and common soap. She stuck a corner of the towel into my ears and gave it a couple of vigorous twists in order to clean out any wax that had built up in them.

'What's this about?' I said to myself. 'Yesterday was Sunday … what's all this fuss about on a Monday?' The answer came to me before long.

'Come on,' said she, taking me by the hand and walking out the front door. 'We have some place to go.'

'Oh! To the shop,' I said excitedly. She didn't answer me.

Down the road we went in the direction of the shop. Something I hadn't thought of was that the school was across the road from the shop. It was when we came as far as Caol Dubh that she spoke her first words to me.

'You're big enough now to go to school. It would be better for you not to be under my feet around the house.'

'But Mam, I'm too small to go to school.'

She looked down on me. 'Yerra, you'll make a lot of new friends at school … children your own age.'

'Will you be with me in school?' I asked her, frightened now.

She looked at me with pity. 'Ah, my love, Mammies are not allowed to stay in school. But you'll have a lovely teacher and she'll be a Mammy to you while you're in school.'

Every day I spent at school, I learned something new. Maybe

it wasn't always lessons that penetrated my skull. To tell you the truth, I wasn't too fond of those same lessons at all, but, unfortunately, I had to make some shape or I'd be in the black books with the school mistress. Within a few months I got to know most of the pupils in my own class, and in the other classes as well. In those days, a child wouldn't be long at school before he was re-christened, that is he would be given a nickname if his family hadn't already got one. One boy in first class was nicknamed 'The Celt'. Another was called 'The Squirt'. I was christened 'Shoot'! That name came to me from my father, Dainín, but how he got it is a long story and I won't go into that now.

There were a couple of boyos in every class. I suppose it should be said that none of us were angels. Not a day would pass that there wouldn't be a fight. If there wasn't a fight behind the schoolhouse, there would be one in Bóithrín na Bruach in the evening. Wait till I tell you about the first fight I got into. Often one of the boys in my class would challenge me to a fight for one reason or another. But no violence followed that first challenge. There was a boy in my class from Cathair Scoilbín – a thin, hardy lad, not as tall as I was but one who wasn't lacking in courage. We spent a long week mouthing at each other, but I hadn't the courage to give him a belt of a fist because I didn't know which one of us would be held responsible. He had a vicious, threatening tongue. One day when we were out at lunchtime, we started arguing. My man with his two hands out in front of him and his fists closed. Not only that, but he had his puss stuck into mine, his every spit going into my mouth with the dint of his rage and arguing.

'It's now or never, Mike Daneen,' I said to myself. We were squaring up to each other for ages and this had to stop some time. My patience had run out. By now most of the boys in our room had gathered around us, some of them egging me on to fight, others egging him on. One of the boys was losing patience with us and couldn't wait for the fight to start. What did he do to start the fight but belt us both in the face at the same time.

'Off ye go now!' I got such a start that I thought it was the other fellow that hit me. I gave him a belt of a fist below the ear that drove him back a couple of feet. But, like a badger, he jumped back at me and landed a solid blow over my eyes. Everyone was cheering and shouting. 'Good man yourself, "Shoot"' from one of the boys. 'Beat the head off him!' from another.

There was a ditch down below the schoolhouse and I thought if I could only get in there, the day would be mine. He landed a couple of blows on my face, but, if he did, he got as good back. I thought, from the amount of blows I landed on him, that I would have him softened up by now. But, alas, it was better he was getting. It would have been better for me to be hitting a cement wall with my fists than to be hitting him. Suddenly, he made a fierce attack on me, but, if he did, I avoided the blow. His legs went from under him, he stumbled and fell. I was going to jump on him, but I didn't. That was the mistake I made! Because, when he got up from the ground, he headbutted me in the stomach and put me on the flat of my back into the ditch. Like a fox attacking a chicken, he was on top of me. His two knees on my belly and he pulling me by the hair of the head. He'd pull my head towards him and he'd punch it as he wished.

'Into school!' The teacher it was who had come to the school railings to call us back to class. It's a bad wind that doesn't blow someone good. Two of the boys laid hands on Tomás and separated us.

'Yerra,' said one of the boys, 'ye'll have to finish the fight another day.'

The two of us were for all the world like two drowned rats that were pulled out of a bog hole. When the mistress saw the state we were in, she lost the head altogether.

'Two tinkers without shame fighting and quarrelling; what would your families say to that? Look at the state of you and you both wet and dirty.'

We got three slaps of the ash stick for our fighting.

'The devil mend us,' said Tomás under his breath, walking back from her table with his two hands under his armpits to relieve the pain in his fingers. 'If we'd kept our cool, this wouldn't have happened at all.'

But a couple of days later the whole thing was forgotten when two more took to the knuckles in Bóithrín na Bruach.

Don't take it that we spent the whole time fighting and quarrelling. Not a day went by, particularly in summer when the sun was high in the sky, that we wouldn't have a game of football. I suppose I shouldn't really call it football because the ball that we had was a small rubber one about the same size as a sliotar you'd use for hurling. That kind of ball was often used for playing handball, too. It was used from third class right down to junior infants. The big boys had a leather football. They used to go to the sand dunes in Feohanagh to play. Out on the road in Moorestown we had our game. This is how the teams were picked. Two boys from third class would stand opposite each other; each in turn would pick a boy for his team until everyone, right down to the last infant, would be picked on one side or the other.

We used stones for goal posts; two stones at the top of the Moorestown Road in from the new roadway and the other two stones beside the angle of the bend. In those days, no car or truck would disturb us because they weren't as plentiful as they are today. Only the odd horse-and-cart went by on its way to Baile Ghainnín Beag Mountain for a rail of turf. We had neither referee nor linesman. The school railing on one side and the school wall on the other. There was no full forward or full back on either team, but everyone following the ball from one goal to the other; that is, everyone except the two goalkeepers.

The goalkeepers were carefully chosen. It was important to be big in order to fill that position because when there was a melee in front of the goals and the other team managed to get the ball over the goal line, they would score a goal. Therefore, it was very important to have a big, strong boy in the gap of danger. That melee would remind you of nothing but a scrum in the game of rugby. One might ask how did that melee come about. Wouldn't it be better for a player to release the ball quickly? Well, that is correct, but if you were any bit slow in releasing the ball, there would be twenty players on top of you in a flash. Then everybody's hands would be fighting for the ball. The person with the sharpest nails for scraping and gouging would come off best. A boy would be making for the goals. Without a doubt you would snap at him in order to stop him, but often you'd get a fist in the face as a result and a goal scored against you into the bargain.

If the ball went over the stone and it wasn't wide or a goal, the goalkeeper would shout 'Over the stone!' and many's the hot argument followed that. As I said at the start, there were no rules in this game. The strongest and hardest of the combatants had their way. There were many disputes about the score, because, as there was no referee, everybody kept the score that was favourable to themselves.

2

The inspector came to our school once a year, usually in November. Don't be talking about the fuss and the flurry that would descend upon the school when we heard that he was coming. We even had to wash and scrub the seats.

We had to clean out the inkwells and shine the brass that covered them. The dust on top of the cupboards had to be cleaned, but the most important thing of all was that each pupil have his lessons off by heart. I remember one particular time the inspector came. We were expecting him for a few days because he had visited the other schools in the area.

Neither her ash stick nor her cocoa spoon was to be seen on the mistress' desk. I figured that she had them hidden away. It was a gloomy, foggy morning when the inspector arrived. We were all sitting quietly, listening to the mistress reading a story from a book she had borrowed from some other teacher. She often did that in order to prepare us for a more senior class. There's no doubt but that she was a first-rate teacher. But what good was that to her when we hadn't our minds set on learning?

A knock came to the door. It was the principal teacher and it was easy to see that he was in a state of panic. The mistress opened the door and they began to speak in whispers. The mistress returned after a couple of minutes.

'The inspector has arrived,' she informed us. 'You will be allowed out in the yard for a while until the inspector is ready to examine you. Don't be shouting and bellowing like beasts. Be nice and quiet and civilised. Then, when the inspector questions you, answer him in a loud, clear voice and don't forget to call him "sir". If you don't, it will be the worse for you.'

Every class in the room was allowed out in the yard even though it was only ten o'clock in the morning. It's a pity the inspector didn't come every day!

After a while the junior infants, senior infants and first class were called in. The rest were told to stay outside a little longer. The inspector was in the middle room. The teachers were at the top of the room beside the inspector who was sitting behind the table, a big head of meat on him, his glasses low down on his nose. When we had all assembled in the room he spoke to us in a pleasant voice.

'By the devil,' I thought, 'maybe he isn't as bad as we were led to believe.'

'I am here,' the inspector began, 'to examine you in preparation for the grant for speaking Irish. But I know that there's no need to question you as you all have fluent Irish. I'll leave it to the teacher to send you to me one by one.'

A girl from Baile an Lochaigh was sent to him first. She was a good scholar. The first question she was asked was what did her father do for a living.

'He's a farmer, sir,' she answered.

'Good girl, Úna,' smiled the inspector. 'How many cows have you?'

'We have five cows, sir,' she replied.

'I suppose,' continued the inspector, 'you have a name for each cow.'

'We have, sir,' she replied.

'Tell me the names of two of the cows,' said the inspector.

She stopped for a minute. 'J-J-Jimmy Terry's cow and the Braddy.'

'Why do you call her the Braddy?' said the inspector.

'Because the first day Daddy brought her home, she jumped the ditch into a neighbour's cornfield.'

'You're a great girl,' the inspector concluded. 'You can go back to your seat now.'

It wasn't long before it was my turn. Up I went before him. The first question he asked me was how many days were in the month of February.

'That depends on the year, sir,' I answered.

'Why is that?' said the inspector.

'Because my father is a seasonal fisherman and he says that February has an extra day every fourth year which is a leap year so that the seasons and the calendar and the moon would be in agreement.' I was released after saying all that.

Things were going just fine until Uinsín Ó Grifín was called up before the inspector. Uinsín was a farmer's son; a quiet, honest boy who never interfered with anybody as far as I can remember. But, like the rest of us, his big ambition was to get the school finished for the day and to head out into the wide world.

'Now,' said the inspector, 'I hear that your father is a storyteller. Maybe you could answer this question: Many's the time a woman cut herself a stick – how would your father finish that statement?'

'Yerra, I suppose it would be hard to put a finish to that,' said Uinsín.

'Why do you say that?' enquired the inspector in high expectation of a proper answer.

'Because that man never answered any question the same way twice.'

'All right so,' said the inspector, 'how would he answer the following proverb, a patch is better than a hole?' Uinsín looked at him, two eyes jumping in his head.

'Sir,' he said, 'somebody asked him that question lately.'

'Well, give us his answer.'

'Aw, I don't know about that, sir.'

The inspector removed his glasses, took a white handkerchief from his pocket and began to wipe them while he waited for Uinsín's answer.

'A patch is better than a hole,' the inspector repeated. Poor Uinsín grew very flustered.

'Oh my! If-if there was a patch on your hole you'd be in a hurry to rip it.'

The inspector looked at the mistress. The mistress looked at Uinsín, and Uinsín looked at the ground. The inspector took a piece of paper that was in front of him and began to write something on it.

'Go back to your seat, Uinsín,' said the inspector.

Ah, if you could only see the mistress. She was wishing the ground would open and swallow her.

'Yes,' I said to myself, 'we'll get the stick tomorrow.'

There were only three others left to be examined and I can tell you that he didn't put any more proverbs in their way, only fine straightforward questions. It was coming up to lunchtime when he finished with us and I can tell you we weren't sorry to have the ordeal over us. He examined the senior classes after lunch. We spent the evening in the yard, happy now that the inspector had come. What other day of the year would we have three lunch breaks? I had a fistful of yellow flag and I was attempting to hit Pádraig Ó Gairbhia with it on the calf of his leg. 'License!' you would say when you hit somebody with the yellow flag and I don't know from Adam where that phrase came from. Just then, the inspector walked out of the school with a leather bag in his hand. One of the teachers was behind him.

'You can go home,' the inspector told us. There was no need to tell us twice. We all went in to the classroom together. One boy was very pleased with himself and he began to sing 'No sums tonight, no sums tonight!' It wasn't long before he got a fist in the mouth and was told to shut up in case one of the teachers heard him.

Towards the end of autumn, a group of tinkers would camp in the waste ground near the school. I think they were of the O'Brien family. We could spend our lives watching the old man among them making saucepans out of tin. I have no doubt but that it was a very special skill. He had made a small anvil specially for the job and a special type of scissors to cut the tin. He had a pointed hammer to flatten the rivets. He had a lovely way of fashioning the bottom of the saucepan and fitting the side around it. Many's the lunchtime a group of us spent on the ditch admiring this craftsman at work. The small canvas tent where they slept was pitched in the shelter of the ditch in order to break any gale that would blow in their direction. They had a blazing fire, and more than a dozen children from three years up to seventeen around it. The tinker's wife wouldn't be seen in the camp during the day, but she would come home about dinner time to cook a bite of food for her husband and the children. She would spend most of the day going from house to house with a big basket filled with saucepans, holy pictures, scapulars, blessed medals and shoelaces. Even though she would sell the goods in her basket, she wouldn't bring it home empty. Because if she sold a saucepan in a house she would ask for a grain of tea or sugar or a drop of milk to bring home to her little ones. Often she came to the school door and, to tell the truth, none of the teachers let her go away empty-handed.

One day, when a crowd of us were perched on the ditch, the

tinker's wife was roasting something on the open fire. Oh boy! The fine smell that was coming to us on the breeze was blowing towards us from Brandon Creek.

'Fresh mackerel,' said a boy near me.

'I suppose they got the fish from the fishermen,' I replied, 'because five or six canoes were in Dooneen last night and each caught more than two thousand mackerel.'

I had but little understanding of the English language, but if you heard the gibberish that came from the tinkers – man, woman and child – it would be as well for you to be listening to Russian. I heard my father saying that the tinkers had their own language and they would use it so that nobody would know what they were saying, only themselves. I'd swear that that's what they were talking on that particular day. There we were, looking at the tinker woman and she roasting the mackerel. I'd say there were at least twenty-five of us boys between big and small, saliva dripping from our teeth. I noticed this big boy a little way from me on the ditch. I won't tell you his name; I had better not for the sake of peace! He had a fine, fat scraw torn by the sole of his shoe from the side of the ditch. The next thing I knew, he had the scraw in his hand. No sooner was it in his hand than I saw it whistling through the air … And where do you think it landed? You're right. Right into the middle of the tinkers' roast. Fish, fat and roasting pot went all over the place. Next, the fire blazed up to the sky because some of the fat had fallen into it. Yes! The damage was done. We scattered east and west, everyone trying to put some distance between himself and the fire for fear the blame would fall on him. The tinker's wife ran after us, yelling and cursing and she didn't stop or stay until she came to the school door. She went into the school and for a while there was no sign of her. Everybody's eyes were on the school door. We didn't have long to wait. The master came out of the school first with the tinker woman close behind him. The master stood at the railing and shouted at us angrily.

'Every boy from sixth class down to junior infants, get inside the school railings immediately.'

Faith! Nobody was in too much of a hurry going into the school yard.

'Hurry up!'

There he was, his head swelled with the rush of blood that came with his fit of temper. When we were all gathered like a flock of sheep in a pen waiting to be sheared, he let out another bark.

'Stand up against the wall all of you!'

It was then we noticed the stick in his hand, rapidly swinging over and back. I was about halfway down the line. Another bark.

'The pupil who threw the scraw, come out here to me.'

Upon my soul, nobody moved. Then he walked to the top of the line.

'You, Kennedy, did you see the boy who threw the scraw?'

'I did not, sir.'

'Hold out your hand.'

He gave him four slaps and with every one he rose half a foot from the ground, the more to put power into the slap. He continued like that down the line, giving the same to everybody. I was thinking to myself while I rubbed my hands together as the master was getting nearer to me that four slaps would be better than to be fleeing from my companions for the rest of the year. We had this kind of code among ourselves: don't tell on anybody, ever. Once upon a time, there were pupils who were only waiting for wind of the word in order to carry stories to the teacher. But there were a couple of boys in sixth class and the informer wouldn't have passed Jack Shea's gate after school before they would be upon him. And God help the informer. Compared to the hiding you'd get from those boys, it was a fine thing to get a couple of slaps from the teacher. That's why they were called the 'Murder Squad'. When the master had gone down through the line, he stood in front of us.

'Do you know that anybody who interferes with the travelling people has no luck for it? They are the Irish that Cromwell evicted out of their houses and land.'

Many funny incidents happened in Moorestown school if I only had to mind to recall them. One day (if I'm not mistaken, I was in first class), the teacher was instructing the junior and senior infants on the natural world around us. She named everything from the mouse to the horse. She named plants and vegetables also. I was more interested in the infants' lesson than I was in the penmanship I was supposed to be doing. She explained cow and calf to them, horse and foal, mouse and baby mouse. When she had finished, she questioned the class to make certain that everybody was listening.

'A question for you, children. The cat is big and the kitten is small. Why are they not the same size? Isn't a kitten a small cat?'

They thrust their hands into the air. Everybody looked as if they had the answer on top of their tongues. But there was one small boy in the middle of the class with his head down. It seemed that he hadn't much interest in what was going on.

'Pádraig,' said the teacher when she noticed him, 'why is the cat bigger than the kitten?'

'Because it is the cat that shits the kitten and if the kitten was as big as the cat, it would make no sense.'

Every child in the room burst out laughing. But the mistress' head wasn't long reddening. She ran down to him and she caught the top of his ear with one hand and the back of his coat with the other. She pulled him out of his seat in one go. Off she went pulling him after her out of the room, muttering to herself with temper.

'I'll teach you, you little blackguard, to leave that kind of talk where you learned it.'

It was easy to know from the screeching and shouting that was coming from the hall that he was getting a good drubbing.

'Stand there for a while and it might teach you your manners,' she said.

She returned to the classroom and continued with lessons, but I can assure you that she put no more questions that day because she got such a start from Pádraig's answer. You could hear a pin drop for a while. We sat there with our heads down, each of us attempting to do the best writing we could. Because we felt in our minds that if even one word was misplaced, we'd get the cocoa spoon across the back of the hand.

3

There were very few conveniences in any house in rural Ireland in the 1950s. Take the parish of Moorestown as an example. The population was about three hundred people living in a hundred houses. There was no electricity, nor even talk of it, in any house. An oil lamp was hung on the wall. There was an open turf fire with an iron crane over it and a big black pot hanging from it for cooking potatoes. If anybody saw a television in those days, he would have it that he saw pookas. There were only two radios in the parish, one in our house and the other in a house at the far side of the parish. They were worked by batteries, one wet, and the other dry. I wouldn't be telling you a lie if I said that the radio we had was as big as the television we have now. We had little interest in some of the programmes because they were in English.

My father and mother would listen to the news every evening and then the radio would be turned off. It was very handy for football matches, particularly the All Ireland. The house would be packed with people on All-Ireland Sunday. Many's the time my father would have to open one of the windows so that the people who were listening in the garden because of lack of room in the house could listen to the match. Nobody in the house was allowed to lay a finger on the control knobs in case one of them would be turned wrong. My father would have his ear pressed to the radio when the news was on. He often fell asleep during the news and the radio would be still on while he snored and snored. Maybe there would have been music that nobody in the house was interested in on the radio after the news. But we were too afraid go near it to turn it off. You'd hear my mother at the bottom of the house shouting 'Turn off "the poorhouse".' Then my father would wake with a start and switch it off. Then he would get a white sheet and cover the radio with it. My parents were afraid that dust would get into it and damage it badly. The poor creatures! They had no concept of the new devices that were coming into the world. Music, greyhounds and football… Three subjects that should not be allowed in any house because all that follows them is disagreement and idleness. The person who thinks only of sport and high jinks never has a thought for house or family. That's how my father would dismiss any argument that arose among us over sport or music. That is not to say that he had no interest in football, because he had; and an interest in music too. He could even play a few tunes on the accordion as we were to find out later on. Like everybody else, he would have his ear to the radio when Mícheál O'Hehir was broadcasting the matches. He'd always have the bad word before a match. 'We won't beat Roscommon today' or 'Mayo will beat us easily': that was the kind of talk he'd go on with. He always fancied the team that were playing against Kerry. My mother would be in such a state if the two teams were on equal scores that she would have to walk out to the garden in case a goal would be scored against Kerry. But that's me all over – talking about football when I was telling you an entirely different story.

Even though we weren't constantly listening to the radio in our house, all the same some programmes left their mark on us, particularly music programmes. The odd play in Irish would be on the radio too, that is to say two or three times a year. Well, seldom heard, much admired. Now and again one of the neighbours would come in to listen to a programme that was mentioned in the newspapers. I well remember one particular night when one of the neighbours, a woman, came to visit. She had no experience of radios or anything pertaining to them. My mother encouraged her to remain for a while to hear a play that was being broadcast that night.

'What use is it to listen to a play,' she replied, 'if you can't see it and the actors on the stage before your eyes?' In the end, she agreed to stay to see how this strange contraption worked. My father was out fishing, and, if he was, the woman was put sitting in his chair to listen to the radio. My mother switched it on a few minutes before the play was due to begin. It was a play in the English language. When it started, everybody fell silent. As the drama progressed, the woman's interest was rising. There she was putting her ear closer and closer to the radio in case she wouldn't hear it properly. We were getting more entertainment out of this poor woman than from the play. Suddenly the dialogue on the radio stopped. She pressed her head closer still to the radio because she thought it wasn't working properly. 'You are near enough now' was the actor's next line. The actor recited the line out loud and, of course, it was part of the play. The poor woman gave one jump out of the chair.

'Oh Jesus Christ! Forever be He praised! How did that fellow see me from the radio?' She caught her shawl that she had left on the back of the chair and she made for the door. 'That thing is no good … it's away with the fairies!' she cried.

The old people's favourite pastime, particularly in the long winter nights, was to go walking to the neighbours for entertainment and gossip. There were many houses in the parish that were renowned for the fine company that used to visit them. There were fine storytellers and the odd comedian among the company. Often somebody would sing a couple of verses of a song. When I say a couple of verses, often they would stretch to twenty verses. The bards, over whom the clay of the graveyard was growing daisies for a few hundred years, had weaved fine Irish into their songs.

One particular man would visit our house at least three nights a week. He would come for the Six o'clock News because at that time the Korean War was raging and, as many from the parish were in America and maybe in the American army, he wanted to know if there was any sign of the war ending. In storm, wind and rain he came regularly. He lived in Moorestown, about a mile down the road. O'Connor was his surname and, as was the custom at that time, he had a nickname. Didn't every dog in the place know 'Grae'? He was a tall, stout, bulky man full of fun and games. He had a large store of stories – funny stories I mean. It was his custom to sit back in a chair until it stood on its back legs only. Then he would have the chair creaking over and back while he smoked his pipe. Now and again he would inhale the smoke deeply into his lungs and blow out the smoke through a gap in his teeth. Because we hadn't enough chairs in the house, often one or two of us would get a fine sod of turf and place it under us near the two legs of the hob for a seat, our backs to the heat that was in the stones since the first day a fire was lit in that place.

I can still picture the way we were all in a line around the fire. In the corner near the cupboard where the radio was kept sat my father, Dainín. Beside him would be my brother Páidí. He was the eldest in the family. I had another brother in America for a few years. Seán was his name. Beside Páidí would be Dónall, then my sister Máirín. Grae would be sitting directly in front of the fire, my mother at his left, and I would be sitting on a sod of turf, my back to the two legs of the hob. I had another brother, Tomás, but he would be put to bed because he would only have been about four at that time.

Grae's stories were mostly about fishing. My father and Grae had spent a long time fishing together in a canoe.

'I remember the morning, Dainín ...' Grae would begin. Every ear would be cocked when he would start with that sentence because we knew that a funny story or a tale of wonder would follow. Without a doubt, the best stories would be kept until the children were sent to bed. But many's the time I listened, my ear to a hole made by a knot in the wood of the door. One night when I was listening there, I heard of the adventure that I enjoyed most. This is how Grae told it.

'By the devil, Páid Carty, Hugh and I were fishing for wrasse out from Cuas na Ceannaine last Thursday. We had crab for bait on our hook. We were winding our line about a fathom from the bottom and we were getting no bite. Then Hugh said to come up a couple of fathoms with the hook. Yes, my fine boy, if we did, it wasn't long before the line was jumping. Within an hour we had twenty wrasse on board and three pollock. The hunger was catching me.

'"Listen lads," I said, "the sea is at low tide now and it won't matter if we pull into the small cave below the Beann. I have small black sods of turf and some fir in my knapsack. We'll boil the wrasse." The two others had the same disease as myself – hunger. We pulled into the little cove. It was my job to light the fire while Carty gutted the fish. The other lump stretched on the sand, sunning himself ...

'"Wasn't it fine and fast you made yourself the boss?" I said to him. But, upon my soul, he had an answer.

'"Only for me, you would be winding that line yet. With

nothing on that hook but bait." So I got my little skillet and put my portion of the fish into it neatly.

'When the fish were boiled I said, "Now lads, I suppose ye have plates." But, no! I was the only one who had a plate. Hugh ran down to the canoe and got a cup we used for bailing out water.'

'Isn't it well the devil thought of it?' said Dainín.

'He did, the bastard,' said the other man, 'but listen a while because that's not the end of the story.'

'Carty ate from the bottom of the skillet. When we had finished eating, Hugh rubbed his belly.

'"The nicest bit of fish I ever ate," he said. "It is best to boil fish in the water they swam in."

'"Listen, Hugh," I said to him, "Is that the cup from the canoe that you were drinking from just now?"

'"It is," said the other man.

'"And did you wash it before you put the fish into it?"

'"I didn't. Why would I do that because the only thing that ever went into it was sea water?"

'Well, that very week Jéimsín and Sayers and myself were fishing with a trammel. We were at least four miles out in the sea. Jéimsín got the runs. Something he ate, I suppose. He had to let his trousers down and put the cup to his backside. I can tell you, he let out a fine load into it. Yerra, Christ! Hugh turned pale with a start and puked up everything he had eaten.'

You would hear my mother and father laughing down in Baile Ghainnín.

'And,' said Dainín, 'did Jéimsín do "the king's deed" into the cup?

'Not at all,' said Grae.

That is only one example of the stories that were told at

the fireside long ago. When one storyteller was finished his story, another would be ready with yet another story. We lived in poverty but, even so, we had plenty of tea and bread, the occasional half a pig's head, plenty of fish and the odd gallon of porter for the grown-ups on special occasions. There was no need for television because we could make our own entertainment.

4

The river that runs by the bottom of our village rises on the side of the hill in Cam an Lochaigh. It marks the boundary between Carrachán and Baile Ghainnín. It is hard for me to give you the name of the river because it is called after each village it flows through. If you were up in Baile Breac, the people there would say that it was the Baile Breac River. If you happened to be in Baile Ghainnín, they would persuade you that it was called the Baile Ghainnín River. Follow the river through the bottom of Moorestown to Feohanagh until it flows into the sea at Feohanagh Strand. Or maybe I should call it Baile Dháith Strand! I suppose if a person were to go outside the villages I have mentioned, it would generally, even officially, be called the Feohanagh River. Some parts of this river are deeper than others.

Any place where the land is level, the water sits dead and the river runs slowly, there is a deep *poll* or hole there as a rule. Every one of these deep holes has a name. For example, the hole that was between Cill Chuain and Baile Ghainnín was called Poll na Leacht. Another hole that was between Baile Ghainnín Beag and Moorestown was called Linn and Chaisleáin. Everybody in Moorestown knew why it was so called: because Moorestown Castle was directly in front of it. 'Moorestown Castle, the Castle of the Five Corners, was the finest castle in Ireland,' the old folk used say. Halfway down in the direction of Feohanagh was another hole which was called Poll Liam … Don't ask me how it got that name!

I suppose there weren't many rivers in Ireland that had as

many fish, considering its size, as were in this river in the 1950s. Because money was so scarce in those years, it was no wonder that some of the fish were poached, that is taken illegally, from the river. My father had a special pike made for this job, and when the fishing season would open you would see him tightening the handle to the top of the pike for fear it would get over stressed during the fishing season. Like any other skill, this particular one, that is salmon fishing, has to be learned when a person is young, as there is a particular knack pertaining to it.

Take your ordinary person walking down the bank of the river. A fish could be right in front of him and he wouldn't see anything but water running with the fall. But the person who was skilled would have his eye that was closest to the water carefully observing the riverbed in towards the bank. Often you would see the top of the water dead, without movement. But it is better for me not to say any more about these things in case too many people would learn them. We used nets too, in the night. Those nets worked in the holes in the river and trammels were best for this job. If a salmon went into the pocket behind the mesh, he would get even more entangled. The mesh on the trammel was small enough to catch white trout also. But the use of the pike needed the most skill. You would seldom get a second chance with the pike because if you failed to spear the salmon at the first attempt, he would go mad after being wounded by the pike.

There were certain people who had the name of being quick with the pike. There were two men living close to us at home and if there was such a thing as a black belt for that skill they would have won it many times. One of them was so renowned that even on the night he was in his coffin, a poacher went by his corpse and said aloud: 'It's an awful pity to put your eyes into the earth. As a matter of fact it's an awful pity to put any part of you into the earth without first finding out how you were moulded.'

If that man were alive, he couldn't have wished for a better prayer over him because the poacher and he were forever in competition with each other to see who was the best poacher.

One day I was walking on the bank of the river from Baile Ghainnín across to Droichead an Chláir. I never crossed that bridge without casting an eye down into the hole above it and I did it again on this particular day. If I did, I saw a sight that raised my heart. Down beside a willow bush he was with his tail moving over and back. 'It's there you are, my trickster, and I nearly didn't see you,' I said to myself. I hurried down Bóthar an Chláir, heading for home. My father was just coming out of some field or other with a donkey on a halter.

'Tie the donkey to that pole for a while,' I said to him.

'What the devil is wrong with you?' said Dainín.

'Oh, there's a salmon in the hole below the eye of the bridge.'

There was no need for me to say any more because, with those words, he released one of the reins that was attached to the donkey's headstall and he tied it firmly to the pole.

'The pike is up in the rafters in the upper cabin. Get it.'

There was no need for him to tell me where the pike was because I had seen it many times before this. I got the pike and it wasn't long before we were trotting down the road towards the bridge.

'Don't run,' my father warned, 'or you'll be noticed in Baile Ghainnín and we'll have help, a thing we don't want for this job.'

We reached the place where I had seen the salmon, but, if we did, hadn't he gone!

'He can't be too far from here,' my father said. I looked down the river and I saw the salmon about six feet away from the place I first saw him.

'Don't say anything,' I whispered, 'he is straight in front of you.' My father prepared himself for work.

'I see him!' he exclaimed. No sooner had he said that than he had the pike stuck in the fish and was pulling him out of the river. 'A fine big one,' my father said. But, just as he spoke, the salmon gave one twist in order to put the pike off him. As if you were closing your eyes, the pike cracked into two halves. With the fright he got, my father fell head first into the hole, his teeth and pipe still in his mouth. Before you could blink an eye, the salmon was gone up the river with the pike and a bit of the handle still stuck in him. I had to burst out laughing. But, if I did, it wasn't long before I stopped because the fellow in the river was getting angry. I had never heard my father use bad language until that day. There he was, his cap gone with the stream, and he'd remind you of nothing but a half-drowned rat. A stream of words came out of his mouth that I didn't think were in the Irish language at all.

But, coming back to the fish. We spent the whole evening searching, but we could find no trace of him.

'Wherever he is now,' said Dainín, 'his belly will be turned up by evening.'

We were just about to give up and walk home when Dainín saw a little stream of blood coming from the green vegetation on the bank of the river. He put his hand into the river and, when he pulled it up, we saw the finest salmon that ever came out of the Feohanagh River. Even though my father was soaking wet, you could see the happiness in his face as he made his way home.

Many's the fine summer evening one of my neighbours and I spent drawing a net up and down the river from Baile Ghainnín Bridge down to Béal na Trá. There was no hollow or rock, hump or barbed wire on both sides of the river that we didn't know. The police kept watch over the river in those years, but often a bailiff who was a stranger would come around too. It was seldom a net would be taken out by day as it would be too hard to hide if the police or bailiffs came after us. Even when we were fishing by night, we would always have a scout at the bridge closest to us, and, if he saw any car that made him suspicious, he would whistle twice, thereby giving us time to pull in our net and hide it in a hedge or suchlike or in a gullet on the bank of the river and then run like the hammers of hell. Everybody made their own way home when the chase was on. You would think nothing of having three or four nets in the river at the same time as long as there was a good distance between them. We believed that the river belonged to everybody in the parish.

In the year I am talking about there were so many salmon and white trout in the river that, to get a week's supply, you only had to fish the one hole. It was easy to find buyers for them as there were many strangers on holiday. Some of the visitors would give their right hands for a fresh fish, and, when the fish was a salmon, it was even better. If the fish weren't sold to the visitors, we would go to the hotels in Dingle. Without a doubt, the hoteliers knew that the fish weren't legally caught and so they bought them cheap. Salmon were so plentiful in 1946 that I remember a fine fourteen-pounder being sold for twelve shillings. But what matter? We had pocket money.

5

I suppose I was twelve years old when I smoked my first cigarette. I often used to stand at the gable of Tigh an Phoirt in
Feohanagh because that is where everybody, young and old,
used to gather in the evenings. Anybody who had reached the
age of sixteen would have a butt of a cigarette between his lips.
It was a sign that you had come of age back then to smoke a
cigarette in public. I would stand beside anybody who had a
Woodbine in his mouth. I would stand on the windward side
so that the smoke from the cigarette would be wafting by my
nose. Oh boy! There was a fine smell from that smoke. Now and
then we'd get a drag from one of the men, but that was seldom
as some of them hadn't the price of the cigarettes. When they
had about half the cigarette smoked, they would put out the
red burning part on top of it to spare the cigarette for another
time and they would put it back into their pockets. Then they
would light the stub after a while. You would be watching out
for anyone who had a box of cigarettes.

However, you wouldn't be looking for a whole cigarette at
all, only a butt. A person wasn't a man, in our opinion, until
he had a fag in his puss and he letting out the smoke down
through his nose. There was a kind of bravado about cigarettes
in those days, or so we thought. There was one boy in Moorestown, his name was Eddie Hutch, and he wouldn't come to
school any day without the butt of a cigarette in his pocket. I
questioned him one day about this.

'My uncle Mike gives me a lot of fags,' he said.

It wasn't long before I made the odd trip to uncle Mike to become better acquainted with him! I had a desire for cigarettes and he was generous with his. One fine Saturday at the end of summer I went to visit him over in Moorestown. I went into Hutch's house where Mike was sitting in the corner in a *súgán* chair with Eddie on a stool beside him and a cloud of smoke coming from the both of them.

'Sit down, my boy,' said the uncle, pointing his cane towards a little stool that was under the table. I wasn't long sitting down when Mike produced a box of cigarettes. My heart rose.

'Have you the bad habit yet?' he enquired.

'He has,' Eddie told him, taking a cigarette out of the box before I could make any reply. He stuck the cigarette into my mouth, took a coal from the fire with the tongs and reddened the cigarette. It wasn't long, I can tell you, before I was making smoke as well as the other two. The rest of the household had gone to Dingle and so the three of us had the freedom of the house.

'Inhale the smoke,' said Eddie, 'or you'll get no satisfaction from it.'

I did, thinking I was as good as any man with the cigarette between my fingers. When I had half the cigarette smoked, I put it out as good as any grown man. I stayed like that until I felt my head getting light and my lungs taking a bad turn, or so it appeared to me.

'I must go home to bring in the turf for the morning,' I said, running out the door and rising dust from the ground in my haste. I legged it back as far as a disused side road that was covered with bushes. 'Bóithrín an Bhy' we used to call it. I found a spot there where nobody could see me and puked my guts out. I lay there for an hour in the hope that I would recover from my sickness. I thought I was on my last legs. After a while I started to come to myself and I headed home.

You would have thought that would have been a lesson to me, but the proverb says that sense doesn't come before age and that's the way it was with me, too. I kept on smoking the odd cigarette here and there and it wasn't long before I was addicted. It was seldom I had enough money to buy cigarettes because if I earned any few pence working with farmers I would have to give it to my mother. Life was hard in those days and money was scarce at home. On Monday mornings Eddie and I would go to the parish hall. We would both have a small tin box as there would be a lot of cigarette butts outside the hall door after the Sunday night dance. We would take the paper from the butts and put the tobacco into the boxes. Then we would hide the boxes in a hole in the ditch near the Caol Dubh, and, if we wanted a smoke during the week, all we had to do was have a few strips of the *Kerryman* newspaper in our pockets and a handful of red 'Friendly' matches.

A packet of Woodbines cost ten pence ha'penny and a box of matches cost three ha'pence. I can tell you that it was harder to come by that shilling then than to come by a five pound note today. When we hadn't cigarettes, we did without them. We had many plans to come by the price of cigarettes. Many's the time a couple of us would pay a visit to horses' stables in the dead of night where we would cut the hair from the horses' tails and, sometimes, from the mane as well. We would do this particularly if a tribe of tinkers were around because they would pay a shilling per pound weight for horses' hair. Of course, the tinkers got the blame when the horses' tails were seen cut to their stumps. But people used to cut the hair from horses' tails long before we took to doing it. I well remember Dainín telling us about the night long ago when John Horgan's mule's tail was cut. The prayer his wife let out of her the following morning when she saw the mule's tail and the state it was in was:

'Whoever cut the mule's tail, may he not live to see the hair grow again.'

'Twas no fun to be playing with a woman like that.

Another plan we had to come by cigarette money was to raid henhouses. A couple of eggs here and a couple of eggs there and you had a dozen. You'd get a shilling and nine pence for a dozen eggs. You wouldn't raid the henhouses in Carrachán because they were built on to the dwelling houses. There was an old man in Carrachán and he was forever around his house. It would be easier to break into Fort Knox than to get into his yard. 'Meex' was his nickname, and I don't know in the face of the earth where he got it.

I remember spending one long morning examining his yard from the shelter of a ditch. He would feed the hens himself when he let them out in the morning. They would come out through a small hole in the bottom of the door. There was room for only one hen at a time. He would wait for the hens as they came out. He would catch them one by one and stick a finger under their tail feathers and up into the place of the eggs. Any hen who had an egg according to this examination, he would put at the other end of the yard where he had nests prepared for laying hens. The finger that Meex used to stick up into the place of the eggs was twisted in such a way that you would think it was specially designed for the job. You'd say to yourself that you'd have your work cut out to make the price of a packet of fags in that place.

I can tell you that eggs got me in a tangle one time and it was in no chicken run I found them. One day when I was walking at the bottom of our own garden I happened to go on top of the ditch. There was a furze bush near me on the ditch and, whatever noise I made, out came a hen – one of our own – and you would think from the racket she was making that there were one-and-twenty in pursuit of her. I examined the bush and, if I did, I came upon a nest with at least a dozen eggs in it. I stopped a while looking at the eggs. The hen was a good bit from the nest, cackling madly. I counted the eggs; there were thirteen of them. What was going through my head was the fine smoke I'd have tomorrow because of them. How used my mother clean those eggs? Oh, yes! With the soda she kept to put in the bread to make it rise. I went up the garden towards the house, whistling to myself so that nobody would notice the hurry I was in.

There was no one in the house when I got there and I took some of the soda from the jar where my mother kept it. I got my mother's message bag and put a few pages of an old Kerryman newspaper into it. When I had that much done, I headed for the eggs again and when I came to the nest, that old devil of a hen was in it. I put in my hand to take out the eggs but, if I did, the hen caught me with her beak and knocked a good peck out of me. 'Bad cess to you, you bitch,' I shouted, catching her by the tail and flinging her from me halfway up the garden. Then I put the eggs carefully into the bag and took them down to the river bank. I rubbed soda on each one of them and washed them in the river. I put a twist of paper around each egg and put them neatly back into the bag. I headed for the creamery where they used to buy eggs, but I didn't go down the road; instead I took the short cut through the fields because I knew that my father was gone for a creel of turf and I didn't want to meet him! I gave the eggs to the creamery manager and he paid me on the spot. Yes! I was thinking to myself, I'll have fags for a week.

A few evenings later I was sitting by the fire while my mother was setting the table for supper.

'I wonder,' said she, 'why is the creamery manager visiting us this evening?'

My heart jumped up to my mouth and I jumped too. I had one eye on my father who was in the corner, clouds of smoke coming from his pipe. I had my other eye on the door. It wasn't long before it opened and the creamery manager walked in. He had a bag in his hand and he placed it carefully on the table. I took the empty turf bag that was at the bottom of the house.

'I must bring in a bag of turf,' I blurted.

'Wait a minute,' the creamery manager said. 'The eggs you sold me a couple of days ago …'

'What eggs?' enquired my mother, looking surprised. 'I didn't send you any eggs for three weeks.'

There I was, a good few yards of the kitchen between me and the door. 'I'll get a right doing now,' I said to myself.

'It was Mike who brought them to me yesterday morning, I sent them into Dingle Creamery and, when they were put under the egg tester, there were chickens in eight of them and four of them were glugars. All the chickens were dead in the eggs.'

My father gave one jump out of his chair in the corner and hit me a belt in the ear.

'Where did you get those eggs?' he demanded.

'In-in-in the nest at the bottom of the garden.' I got up, but no sooner had I got to my feet than he made for me again. Every blow I got was like a blow from a sledgehammer.

'What did you do with the money?'

'I bought chocolates and sweets.'

'And did they give you the diarrhoea?' he said, taking me by the back of my coat. I was near the door by now and my coat was slightly too big for me. I slipped out of it and left Dainín inside the door with the coat in his two hands. I tore off down the garden in the direction of the river as fast as my legs would carry me and hid in Inse Bhaile Ghainnín until the storm would die down. Night was falling and I was afraid to face home. After a while I noticed somebody approaching the Inse.

'Are you there, Mike?' It was my brother Páidí.

'I'm here beside the ditch,' I replied. 'Where's Dad?'

'He's gone fishing,' Páidí informed me.

'Oh, thanks be to God. Is Mam still mad at me?'

'She said you'll have nothing to fear if you come home.'

When I got home I was given tea and bread. 'Now,' said my mother, 'I hope you've learned a lesson today. When you come home from school tomorrow, you'll have to split a bag of potatoes for seed to make up for the price of the eggs.' That didn't go down too well with me because there was nothing I hated more than to be splitting seed potatoes, because neither God nor man could split them to please Dainín.

6

I was drawn to the accordion more than to any other instrument. Well, I liked every instrument but my heart was set on the accordion. While I am speaking of music, it is as well for me to tell you the story of how the first accordion came into our house. This programme used to be on the radio once a week; it was ballads and traditional music that were on it. The sponsors of the programme were a company in Kildare that used to sell musical instruments. If I remember rightly, they called themselves 'Cox of Kilcock'. They sold instruments made by the Hohner company. I didn't have the opportunity to hear as much music as I would have liked. There wasn't a tape recorder, nor talk of one, in any house. The odd house had a gramophone, but they were few and far between.

The only other chance I had to hear music was when I was on the roads around Feohanagh after mass. There was a musician by the name of Seán Ó Dómhnaill who lived below the creamery in Feohanagh. Often a crowd of boys would gather outside his house, myself among them. Some of the boys would be throwing pennies on the road, more would be talking, but I would always have my ear cocked listening to Seán if he happened to be playing music.

There was a certain magic in his music and he had such a large store of tunes that you would think that nobody could keep them in his head. Seán used to play in Arús Bhreánainn at that time – himself and Muiris Ó Cuinn from Corra Ghráig. Muiris was a good musician too, a man who had music in his feet as well, not to mention a fine singing voice. If you were to meet him today, he is every bit as musical as he ever was, God bless him.

My brother Páidí was working for the County Council in Ventry Quarry about this time and he was as interested in music as I was. He had better opportunities to listen to various musicians as he used to go to the dances. About this time, Muiríoch Hall opened and dance bands came from all over to play there. One fine summer evening, Páidí and I were sitting on the ditch outside our house talking about a musician who had come home from England.

'Ah, Mike, if you could only hear the tunes he has and the way he plays the two rows of the accordion together.'

'Tell me, Páidí, what make of a box has he?' I enquired.

'Wait a minute until I think. Oh yeah, Paoli Scragini ... No, it isn't but a Paoli Soprani, or some kind of a name like that,' Páidí informed me.

'Oh Holy Mary,' I exploded after a while, 'Wouldn't it be nice if we had an accordion ourselves?'

'Yerra,' said Páidí, 'Where would we get money to buy something like that?'

'I was listening to the radio a couple of days ago,' I continued, 'and Cox of Kilcock had a programme on it. They are a company up in Kildare who sell musical instruments. They sell accordions made by Hohner. I wonder if that make is any good? This man was talking about the Hohner double row. Twelve pounds, ten shillings and sixpence is the price of it, but if a person had two pounds to put down he'd only have to pay twelve shillings and sixpence a month to clear the balance.'

'And how would we know what kind of a box it is without seeing it?'

'Oh,' I replied, 'you can get a book with pictures of the accordions and the price of every one.'

Páidí was thinking for a while.

'Listen,' he said, 'I'll give you the price of the stamp if you send away for that book.'

All I wanted was wind of the word. The following day, I posted the letter. After a few days, we got a reply. I waited until Páidí came home before I opened the letter.

We studied the whole catalogue carefully.

'Isn't that the box you mentioned?' Páidí said in the end. 'And, my word, isn't it a beauty? Mark it.'

Late that night my father went walking to Jer Fada's house. We were all gathered around the fire and my mother was in great humour.

Páidí spoke: 'I make out that if there was an accordion in this house, it wouldn't take me or Mike long to bring music out of it.'

'As you're talking about accordions,' I added, 'they are on sale on the radio every week and they cost next to nothing.'

My mother rose from the chair. 'They'd want to cost next to nothing before you could buy one,' she said.

Páidí jumped into the conversation then. 'You only have to put down two pounds and pay twelve shillings and sixpence a month until the balance is cleared. Listen, Mam, I'm working and I would have that twelve and sixpence a month.'

'I won't stop ye, but, God save us when Dainín hears it – he'll make ructions,' said my mother.

'But, Mam,' I implored, 'where will we get the two pounds to put down?'

'I'll give it to ye,' said Mam.

I let out a shout, jumped from the chair and put my two hands around her.

'Yerra, Mam, you'll have no trouble coming around Dad,' I assured her.

Yes, we sent for the accordion and, after waiting patiently, a letter came informing us that it would be sent to Ballydavid Post Office. I brought it home. When I arrived at the house, the rest of the family were waiting to feast their eyes on this wonderful contraption. I laid the parcel the accordion was wrapped in on the table. No sooner was it on the table than I was given a sharp knife to hurry things up. I wasn't long taking the cord and the wrapping paper from it.

'Ah, boy, lying there in that box, the instrument that warms the cockles of my heart,' I exclaimed.

I took it out of its box and laid it on the table. I put the straps around my shoulders after the accordion had been examined by everybody. Off I went, pushing and pulling and pressing the buttons. But, alas, the noise I brought out of it was far from music.

'Give me that a minute.' It was my father who spoke; he had just come in from the bog.

'What's this? You'd shape a sod of turf better than you'd bring a tune out of that instrument,' I said to him.

He took it from me. My father had two hands that were as wide as the blade of a shovel and he had short, thick fingers. It was always said that long, slender fingers were the first sign of a good musician. He started going up and down through the buttons of the accordion. Upon my soul, after a while he started to string a couple of notes together and I had been thinking up to then that he hadn't a note in his head.

'What tune is that, Dad?' I asked him. He looked at me with a smile on his face.

'That's "An Bóthar ó Thuaidh chun Trá Lí",' he informed

me. And that wasn't the only tune he had. Well, I never saw the likes of it. My father able to bring music out of an accordion.

'I'm married to that man with more than twenty years,' exclaimed my mother, 'and I didn't know he had a tune in his body.'

He had to play the few tunes he had five or six times.

'Where did you learn your music?' I asked him after a while. You'd think it was Jimmy Shand I had for a father.

'Yerra, Seán Coughlan and I were staying in the same house in Chicago and I used to get the odd go on his accordion,' he informed me. After tea, I faced my room to see if I could make any hand of it. God save us, there was some noise from that room. After a while, I got the first two notes of 'Ar Maidin Moc', but by that time I was sweating from all the pressing and pulling.

Out in the night, the box was given to my father again and it was Páidí's turn to wonder at the fine music we thought he was playing. My father was the hero of that night anyway.

Every night, after I had taken a quick glance at my lessons, Páidí and I would go down to the room. After a fortnight we had a couple of tunes learned, or so we thought. One night my mother was in Dingle and who should be on the bus home with her but Seán Coughlan from Arda Mór. Seán is a fine musician who played for years in the big dance halls of Chicago. My mother was telling him that we had a new accordion in the house. It wasn't too hard to coax him off the bus at the top of Bóthar a Bhuitsir, as trying out new musical instruments was always dear to his heart. He wasn't long in the house when I was told to bring the accordion down from the room to allow a real musician to try it out. Seán handled the box expertly and it was plain that he knew what he was doing. Oh, he was a fine, skilful player. He played a difficult, complicated reel – one I hadn't heard previously. I suppose, I said to myself, that I'll never see the day that I will be able to play as fast as Seán. My head was getting light with every tune he played and my feet were beating time to the music on the floor. He stopped after a while.

'What is the name of the last tune you played?' I enquired of him.

'The name that is given to that tune, my young boy, is "Stocaí Breaca John Mhicil".'

'I thought there were two tunes, one after the other,' I ventured.

He laughed. 'Oh, house don't fall on me,' said Seán, 'you have a good ear for music. "Cnagarnach na Cairte ar an mBóthar" is the name of the second tune.'

My mother gave him a mug of tea and a plate of meat. While he was eating, I took the accordion and played a few tunes. When I had been playing for a while, Seán spoke to me.

'You're learning on the press instead of on the draw and there's a better way than that to play. You'll have to play the two rows together and you won't have as much pulling on the bellows.'

He spent an hour giving me valuable tips and I can say without any exaggeration that it was Seán who put me properly on the road of music. I thought that this skill wouldn't be as easy to learn as I first imagined. He played a tune I knew myself in the style he was demonstrating to me, and, from that evening on, I never looked back as far as playing the accordion goes.

7

For the last two years I spent in Moorestown School, my father and mother did everything they could to keep me at the books. They wanted me to do the examination for the teachers' preparatory college. At that time, every parent wanted to make teachers of their children.

'Look at the life you'd have as a teacher,' my mother would say to me. 'You'd be finished work at three o'clock every day. You'd have a white shirt and a tie. Can't you see the fine, well-fed condition they all have?'

That's the talk I used to hear every evening after school. 'Go down to the room and do your lessons,' was what was said to me. Maybe I would go down to the room, but, if I did, it wasn't lessons that worried me, but tunes for the accordion.

'Just think of it,' I would say to myself, 'six years in college and my head stuck in some book or other all the time. Holy Mary, it would break my heart and my health.'

I would get pins and needles down my back any time I thought of it. I pretended at home that I was doing my utmost. But I would prefer to be six feet down in a trench with a pick-axe in my hand.

Anyway, I sat the examination, I and a good part of my class. I had no need to wait for the results because I knew in my heart what the result would be.

'Was the exam hard?' my mother enquired in the evening when I returned home. So that she wouldn't be looking for a good result, I told her that it was the most difficult examination ever.

'Yerra,' said she, 'they only want a very few to succeed; teachers' children and the like who are well off.' I was well satisfied with that answer.

'Prepare yourself, so, to go to the Tech in Dingle after the summer. It is enough to have your father under my feet without having you around the house as well.'

Oh boy, my heart almost stopped. 'God knows,' I said, 'I'm not going to the Dingle Tech or any other school because I'm going to go working for some farmer. My heart is broken from books and may God not praise the man who thought of school the first day ever.'

That was when she got mad altogether. 'Right so,' she exploded, 'go working for a farmer and be a slave of the shovel for the rest of your life, working for thirty shillings a week and getting nothing to eat from them when you're going around the place as a wandering farm labourer.'

When my mother got something into her head, neither God nor his Blessed Mother would get it out of it.

'If you want to stay in this house,' she told me, 'it would be better for you to make up your mind to do as I tell you.'

I had to say something myself.

'Oh, God save us, just when I thought I was finished with the books. Look what you're doing to me. 'Twould be better for me to throw myself off of a cliff. There will be nothing in my head but the height of nonsense. Couldn't I make a pound anywhere with a shovel?'

I went out the door boiling with temper. After a while I enquired from another boy who was going to the Tech as to what kind of a place it was. I was glad to hear that there was no comparison between it and primary school. He told me that carpentry and the likes were taught there and that there wasn't the same emphasis on the books. The upshot of this was that I gave in to my mother's talk and made my mind up to try the Tech for a year.

I was fourteen years old at this stage. One fine day after the summer, I walked up to the top of Bóithrín an Bhuitsir from where I was to be transported to Dingle.

I wasn't long waiting when I saw an old banger of a car coming towards me, smoke belching from it as well as an awful noise. It stopped beside me. The man behind the steering wheel was stocky, middle-aged with a gentle looking face. He spoke to me in English: 'Are you going to the Tech?' he enquired. I jumped into the old car. If I remember right, the car was an American make – a Buick, I think. There were three lines of seats in it. At first there were only two rows as in any car, but an extra seat was added – a wooden one. He headed the car in the direction of Ballyferriter. He went over the Seana-Chnoc, south through Ventry and into Dingle. By the time we got to Ventry, there were eleven of us in the car. We looked like nothing but a crowd of hens in a box. But this didn't bother us as we had fine company and a drive around the countryside.

The first thing I noticed about the Tech was that the classroom was in no way like the one we had in the primary school. There were fine wooden benches in it and attached to each bench was a box full of carpenters' tools – a saw, a hammer, a mallet and such like. The girls went into their own room. When everybody was sitting in a bench, two men came into the classroom.

'I am Tomás Ó Cofaigh, the school principal,' one said, 'and the subjects I will be teaching you are Irish, English and mathematics. This is Mícheál Ó hIarnáin here beside me, and he will be teaching you woodwork and mechanical and woodwork drawing. It will be two years before you sit your first examination, the Group Certificate.'

'If we stay here that long,' I said to Seosamh MacGearailt from Clochán Dubh who was sitting beside me.

We spent most of that first morning looking at tools and finding out what they were for. We had an hour for lunch and we weren't forbidden to go into the town of Dingle. Three of my schoolmates from Moorestown National School were going to Dingle Tech with me.

That first day when we were going up Green Street, one of the boys asked us a question: 'Does anybody know where Mikeín Fuacht's house is?' He got no answer. 'If you don't, you soon will,' said this small boy from Glaise Beag. With that, he turned in the door of a house that was a little way down from the Chapel. We followed him. There was a counter inside the house with a small, neat man behind it, mending a shoe. I suppose he had fifty shoes to mend if he had one. They were on the shelves, on the window and some more were thrown into boxes. The shoes he had mended, he put neatly into a corner.

'How are you, Pádraig?' he said.

He knew the boy who brought us in. We were introduced to Mikeín and shortly afterwards Pádraig took a packet of ten Woodbines out of his pocket.

He gave one to me and to the other boys, lit one himself and stuck it into Mikeín's mouth. In a short time, a crowd of boys from the Tech had gathered and you'd know from the man of the house that he was very fond of the youth and that he got great pleasure from their company.

Pádraig told us that he had to bar some of the boys the year before as they were playing tricks on him.

No day would go by from then on that we wouldn't pay a

visit to the shoemaker, except on Thursdays when the shops in Dingle had a half day and they would be closed in the evening. Thursday was the day we played football in the Tech. Up in Páirc an Ághasaigh, we used to play. Ten-a-side and a sub on the line. To tell the truth, it didn't matter if the sub was there or not.

But we'll leave that as it is. Mícheál Ó hIarnáin, our wood-work teacher, was the referee and, because he hailed from Galway, he had a great interest in football. He spoke Connemara Irish and, because we had no recourse to that dialect, we used to get great amusement out of certain words he used. Raidió na Gaeltachta wasn't there at that time nor any talk of it. It was a source of wonder to us that there was another place in Ireland that had Irish and yet it was different to the Irish we spoke. The Galway man was very pleased with the standard of football we were playing after he had been with us for a couple of weeks. It was the highest thought in his head to have a team from the Tech in the county vocational schools' championship.

'Maybe we won't have a team this year but with the help of God we'll have one next year,' he used to say while he was training us.

It is hard to believe, but, after I had spent a couple of months in the Tech, I was getting satisfaction from my schooling for the first time ever. I suppose the reason for this is that I was working with my hands three days a week. I was getting on reasonably well with drawing also. Even mathematics weren't coming too hard to me. The boys there couldn't have been more natural. I suppose the most important thing the Tech gave the boys and girls was the courage to face the great world outside. We had a little more confidence and we also saw how the people of the big town were living.

Canoe races were all the go in those years. Four years before this, the crew from Cuas won the big race in Dingle. Our wood-work teacher used to row canoes in his native county he would tell us. It wasn't too hard, then, to convince him that the Tech should enter for the under eighteen canoe race in Fenit which was to be held in May. We got the loan of a canoe from the man who was working in the lighthouse at the mouth of Dingle Bay. They talk about putting fishing canoes racing today. Well, the canoe we got was a fishing canoe, but the story wouldn't be so bad only her frame was crooked from old age and neither God nor His Blessed Mother could keep her straight if there was any breeze.

'The heavy canoe will strengthen your arms and legs,' the Galway man used to say to us. He was going to try us out in Fenit and, if we did reasonably well, we would make a racing canoe in school as part of the curriculum! He contacted Murt O'Leary in Leith-Triúch and he promised to give us a racing canoe. They had a crew entered for the big race. After spending a couple of months training with the old canoe, we picked the crew who would go to Fenit. The crew were Pádraig MacMathúna from Glaise Bheag, Pádraig Ó Séaghdha from Moorestown, Pádraig Ó Sé from Gleann Fán and myself. That was the seventh day of May, 1957 – a dirty, misty day. The sea was quite rough too.

When we got to Fenit, we looked for Murt O'Leary and it wasn't long before we found him down at the slip. He showed us the canoe riding on the water beside the quay.

'There it is, be careful because it's unsteady,' he warned us.

We stripped to the waist and got in. We rowed a way out to sea to get the feel of the canoe. She was as light as a feather compared to the old thing we were training in. But she went all over the place when we were pulling with the wind. Soon we were called to the starting line. There were five canoes entered for the under-eighteen race. The starter's gun was fired and off we went, rowing with all our might. We had the wind to our backs out to the first buoy and it would have been better for us if we hadn't as we had no experience in handling a racing canoe as yet. We were a good way behind when we rounded that first buoy. We turned directly into the wind then and, as any racing man knows, it is easy to keep a canoe straight against the wind. We put our backs into it and before long we were catching up with the other canoes. We passed the fourth canoe. Now our training with the old canoe was standing to us. We passed the third canoe and we were catching up on the second one with only the length of a canoe between it and the leaders. But, God help us, there were only about twenty yards between us and the finishing line. There was yelling and shouting from the quay and the crew from Fenit carried the day. One of them was so exhausted after the race that he got a weakness.

Well, we didn't win but we gave a good account of ourselves. The teacher was very pleased with us.

'Yes,' he said, 'we'll make a racing canoe for the coming year.' We started to make the canoe the week after the race. We made it after the Galway fashion as 'Timber Mike', our teacher, was from Galway. We gave up many of our Saturdays in order to speed the work. We would cycle to Dingle, and, on top of that, we would put in a long day's work. It was no wonder that we had the canvas on it before Christmas 1957 and it was on a stage above the Tech waiting for fine weather so that we could put tar on it. The day we put it on the water, an uncle of Pádraig MacMathúna was at the jetty watching it cut through the water. This was a man that was on the Dúinín team twenty years before.

When we came back to the jetty after giving it a course

around the bay, one of the boys put the question to him: 'Has she a race in her?'

He pushed his cap back on his poll.

'I don't think so because she's drawing too much water in her wake.'

Needless to say, the four of us got sour and we weren't going to surrender to that kind of talk. And, after spending a long time training for Fenit, we faced the race with hope and confidence in ourselves. But, my grief, we finished last in the race. Yes, it was then that we took heed of what the old man had said. I suppose it wasn't taken from the stage three times after that. It is said that it finished up being bought by a fisherman in Ventry. It is said that same fisherman said it was the steadiest fishing canoe he ever had.

In November 1957, the inter-county football championship for technical schools began. From the previous summer we had been training hard. We played matches against the Brothers' school in preparation for the championship. The number of boys in the Tech was down to seventeen after the summer: fifteen for the team and two subs. It would be disastrous for us if any of the first fifteen got hurt, as God help us if we had to depend on either of our two subs. One of them was good enough at catching the ball but when he kicked it, it went straight up in the air. When the ball would be making for the other sub, he would have his two hands spread out in front of him. He would give a big, high jump so as to catch it, but he was as likely to catch the head of the player near him as to catch the ball. It was said he was short-sighted, but, for all that, we had fifteen fairly good footballers. I would say that seven of our fifteen were as good footballers as any of their age in the county.

Word came to our school that we were drawn against Castleisland in the first round of the championship. The game would be played in Castleisland. 'Timber Mike', our trainer, wasn't too pleased about that. As he said, it was like going into a fox's den playing a team in their own field. We travelled to Castleisland by bus on that wet winter's day. Our trainer gave us a big, long speech on the way. By God! But you'd find yourself getting stronger with every sentence that came out of his mouth. After travelling many long miles of the road, having left many small villages behind us, we got a sight of the outskirts of a big town.

'Look at the spire of the church,' somebody said, 'we're almost there.'

The bus turned left at the top of the town and, about a quarter of a mile out the road, we came to the football field. As we walked down the side of the field, I overheard one of the boys saying to 'Timber Mike':

'We complain about Páirc an Ághasaigh, but it is like Croke Park compared to this mountain of mud.'

We togged out in the corner of the field. When we ran on to the playing field, the other team was already out on it, kicking the ball into the north goals. My heart got a lift when I saw them.

'By the devil,' said Caoimhín Ó Fearaíl, our full forward, 'we have it because they're only small, weak things and I make out that we're a lot stronger than them.'

I was the goalkeeper as the other goalkeeper we had failed completely against the Brothers' School. I wasn't too pleased, I can tell you. I always preferred to play in the forwards. Pádraig MacMathúna, a strapping, strong boy, and Mikeí Doyle Ó Caomhánaigh, another capable footballer with a badger's grip on a ball in the air; they were our two midfield players. The forward we most depended on was Jim Choráilí Ó Beaglaoi from

Cill Maolcéadair. He could put a ball into your eye, he was so accurate. Another player who was as cute as a fox was Bertie Ó Coileáin from Dingle. Peats MacGearailt was a strong, stocky boy who would think nothing of going through a cement wall. In our half-back line we had Tomás MacCárthaigh, a nippy player who would follow his man even if he went out over the ditch. Pádraig MacSíthigh from Dingle was a tall, hardy boy who had all the antics of a footballer and a great sweep for the ball. Pádraig Ó Sé from Fán: he was hard and bony and strong and I pity any player who went shoulder to shoulder against him because I can tell you that he'd be sore after the game. Seosamh Jamesie MacGearailt from Clochán Dubh – a nephew of Joe Siobhán MacGearailt who was captain of Dublin a couple of years previously – a lad who never left a forward inside him, ever. That's some of our team.

The penny was tossed and we played against the wind for the first half. The whistle was blown and the referee threw in the ball. Off with them after the ball. One man lashing it down the field, another lashing it up. Both teams sizing each other up. A couple of balls came into the square in front of me. I let out a few shouts and roars at my backs.

'Is it that these weaklings are too fast for you?' I said to them.

Pádraig Ó Sé was nearest to me. It wasn't worth my while for me to open my mouth because shortly afterwards a high ball came into the left corner. The boy he was marking was under it. Pádraig gave a running jump and rose up behind him. The poor fellow came down on his mouth with his teeth in the mud and Pádraig cleared the ball out to midfield. Upon my soul, but that trullout took the legs from the unfortunate boy and he was afraid to go anywhere near the ball after that.

It wasn't long before their trainer shouted from the sideline:

'Are you afraid of him? Keep in with him – he won't bite you.'

But, if he did, he wasn't long in getting his answer: 'Are you sure he's not one of the teachers? I swear he is shaving for the last seven years.'

Our players settled down after that and played proper football. Would you believe it? No ball came beyond our midfield from the first ten minutes until the whistle was blown for half time. I was standing in the goals, frozen with the cold. I asked our trainer to put somebody else into goals for the second half because I was fed up with standing there. We were so far ahead that it didn't make any difference, and he obliged me. I went in to the forwards eagerly, where I warmed myself up before too long. Castleisland scored only two points, and, at the final whistle, we had scored five goals and fifteen points. They were as bad a team as was ever seen on a football field. On our way home, our trainer made another speech on the bus.

'They are the worst team in the county,' he warned us. 'Don't any of you get a swelled head yet.'

Three weeks after that we had to travel to Waterville for the semi-final. Upon my soul, but this game was as easy as the first one. We were only three points ahead at the end of the first half. Our trainer told us to make a shape in the second half or they would surprise us. Anyone would think that we got an injection from a doctor because when the ball was thrown in for the second half Mikeí Doyle fielded it and sent it into the Waterville goals where Jim Choráilí Ó Beaglaoi was waiting. Like a flash, he had it in the net. That broke Waterville's spirit and, from that to the end of the game, we were picking off points at our leisure. We were fine and happy on the way home; Waterville beaten and we in the county final. Exactly a week later, we heard about the other semi-final. Causeway had beaten Tralee Tech who had won the final the previous year. By this time, we were training three days a week, but we weren't training with the ball only; we did speed training too. Some of our backs were heavy and the odd one was smoking tobacco. We won the toss, and the game was fixed for Páirc an Ághasaigh a fortnight later. Word came from the Causeway camp that one of the Kerry footballers, a man by the name of Bobby Buckley, was training them. That didn't exactly add to our confidence, but our trainer said to us that if they hadn't the stuff in themselves, he wouldn't make much difference to them.

Yes! The day of the final came at last, a fine Sunday in the beginning of May with the sun splitting the stones. West Kerry were playing Boherbee in the county senior championship. We would have no lack of support as a large crowd had come to watch that match. Every one of us was playing in the position where he first began. The match was to start at two o'clock. The night before, every time I thought about the match, my stomach got knotted. Well, I wasn't on my own because when I questioned some of my team-mates the following morning, they were just as bad as me. We were wearing the Piarsaigh's jerseys. Out we went on the field, lepping like young calves that were let out of their stall for the first time, some of us kicking the ball into the goals and more kicking it out. I was keeping a sharp eye on the goals at the other end so that I might see the team we were playing against. They dashed out on to the field. Upon my word, but some of them were likely looking men.

'Now, Mike Daneen,' I said to myself, 'you won't be cold in the goals today.'

After a while the referee came out to the centre of the field. He blew a few blasts on his whistle to let the two teams know that the game was about to begin. Causeway won the toss, and elected to play against the wind in the first half.

Causeway had two tall, strong men at midfield. Our trainer called Mikeí Doyle and Pádraig MacMathúna.

'If they outfield you for the first couple of balls, don't try to catch the ball again; break it away from them with your fists. You are playing at home and the wind is at your backs for the first half. They'll be unsettled for a while and maybe you'll catch them unprepared.'

When the ball was thrown in, our two midfielders weren't caught napping. Pádraig MacMathúna rose in the air and, with one hand, knocked the ball nicely down to Mikeí Doyle who kicked it towards the Causeway goals. Backs and forwards rose for the ball in the square. The ball hit the Causeway full back on the chest and bounced away from him to where Jim Choráilí was waiting. You'd think he had it read because he put the ball in the left corner of the goals about six inches under the crossbar. Boy, what a start! That goal gave the rest of the team great courage and, as the old people used to say, every man was two men after that. We were giving Causeway no time to settle. We had scored three goals and nine points before the whistle blew for the end of the first half. I can tell you that 'Timber Mike' was well pleased with us.

'Keep it up in the second half and there'll be no stopping you.'

'Why wouldn't we?' I said to myself, 'Aren't we a lot sharper than them?'

We went out for the second half and it wasn't long started when we heard a powerful, strong man making every shout from the sideline.

'That's Bobby Buckley now,' Caoimhín Ó Fearaíl told me. 'And isn't he a fine man?'

He was running up and down the sideline like a mad bull.

'Hasn't he the fine English?' I said to myself.

'Put Kirby midfield … you are beaten there … and for Chrissake get your act together,' he exhorted them.

Kirby wasn't long at midfield when he started to win ball in the air. When he couldn't field it cleanly, he fisted it towards our goals. That's when the pressure came on me. He let in a big, high ball from the middle of the field. From the way it was travelling through the air, it would fall on directly on the edge of the small square. Our full back, Caoimhín Ó Fearaíl, slipped under the ball when he was backing under it. Here comes their full forward inside him making for the ball. 'Right,' I said to myself, 'if I'm to die, it's death in Ireland for me.' Out I went at speed to meet him coming in and I jumped for the ball. I put up my fist with my knees stuck out in front of me as this strong lump of a lad was coming at me as fast as the wind. I felt the ball connecting with my fist and at the same time our two bodies collided. I saw a thousand stars and when I gathered my senses again, I was on the ground with that big, awkward, heavy lout on top of me.

'Get off me, you jackass,' I said to him.

'I don't know what you said,' he retorted (I was speaking in Irish), 'but you have a knee as sharp and as hard as a pickaxe.'

He got up off me, still holding his hip. It was a habit of mine always to jump for a ball with my knees out in front of me. It was said that a person would gain extra height by jumping that way. The ball went out to the forty yards line and it could just as easily have gone into the net. There were twenty minutes left and Causeway were tearing through the field. Then they scored a great goal and it was like a doctor's injection to them. They started picking off points from forty yards. Our team were falling apart all over the field. Causeway were only two points behind with three minutes left to play. Our trainer instructed some of our forwards to come back to help with the defence but, in spite of that, the Causeway full forward struck the post with the ball twice. 'Twas the will of God that the referee blew the final whistle because, with the momentum they had built up, there was surely another goal in them.

Yes! We had won the county championship. It was the first time Dingle Tech had won that honour, and the last time they would ever win it. We had mighty celebrations in the school that night; a big meal and the presentation of the medals. A month afterwards we sat the Group Certificate examination. We had loads of preparation to do as we had spent a lot of time in football training before that. Most of us were handy enough at woodwork and drawing, but if we failed any subject, we would have no bit of paper to get and we needed that bit of paper in order to be apprenticed to a tradesman. To make a long story short, we all passed the exam and we were delighted that we had completed our two years. I always say that they were the two best years of my life because I got directions in how to make out in the world beyond and it put me on the right road for life.

8

Summer 1958 – Oh boy! – that was some summer. I was fifteen and a half years old and shaving myself with my own razor. Or should I say, I scraped at the cat's fur on my jaw and under my nose. My father said my beard was so weak that it ran before the razor. The odd week's work was to be found with the farmers and shortly the Irish language courses would begin in Muiríoch. I suppose it wasn't for the sake of speaking Irish that I was looking forward to those courses. Not at all, boy, but for the girls that attended them. Yes, girls, girls and more girls. I make out that between three and four hundred students came that year – boys and girls between twelve and seventeen years of age. They used to have a little céilí in the hall in Muiríoch until ten o'clock at night, and every Monday, Wednesday and Friday night they had a big céilí until midnight. The little céilís were free, but you had to pay two shillings to get into the big céilís. I was in right luck that year because there was no musician available to play for the little céilís. I contacted the course director as soon as I heard the news. The bargain I made with him was that I would get thirty pounds for playing at the little céilís for the three months the courses were on, and free admission to the big céilís.

I can tell you that some people were jealous of me because, God help us, often they wouldn't have the two shillings to get into the big céilís. But I was able to walk in past the doorman and salute him independently without putting my hand in my pocket. What's that my father said when the accordion first came into the house? 'A musician never did anything but went around looking for idle fun.' Upon my soul, but he had to listen now. I was saving hay with a farmer in Baile Ghainnín Beag on the day the course began officially. I was going to be on my trial run that evening, playing in Muiríoch Hall for the little céilí. There was a great crowd of helpers in the meadow that same day because it was a four-acre field and there was no machinery or any other contraption to gather the hay in those days. But my mind wasn't on the hay that day and, to me at least, the sun beaming down on us was a long time setting.

It was making for five o'clock that evening when the last wynd of hay was made. There was nothing left to do but to tie down the wynds with a *súgán* for fear of wind and to rake them down. I wonder in the name of God what this raking was for. Often the raking wouldn't yield more than a bundle of hay. But that was the old crowd for you, and they were very thorough. But they didn't understand the hurry that was on other people at all. Yes! I stuck my pike in the ground at nine o'clock and told my father who was beside me that I had to go away.

'Yerra, what's your hurry?' he said to me. 'Wouldn't you wait another five minutes until we have a smoke and we'll be home together.'

'I'm in a hurry because I'm playing in Muiríoch Hall,' I told him.

'Yerra,' he shoved his cap back on his poll and started making a sermon. 'That's right, music and dancing and women … and I suppose you're smoking too.'

I answered him quickly: 'It isn't too far from home I brought the smoking.'

He had his pipe in his mouth with smoke billowing from it. I was thinking that it wouldn't be too healthy for me to be near him after making that attack.

'That's right,' he came back at me, 'go with the life of pleasure. You'll get nothing but impudence from the youth today. If I spoke like that to my father, he'd break the bone of my backside with a kick from his hobnailed boots.'

He was going on like that as I cleared the ditch out of the meadow and all the men were in stitches laughing at him.

I stripped to the waist when I got home. I got a basin full of hot water and soap and if I didn't give myself a good going over, it isn't day yet. Then I got my new trousers and a clean shirt. Under the bed in a box there was a small long slender bottle of Brilliantine. I didn't spare that bottle, but let a big splash of it out onto my hand and rubbed it into my hair. Then I started to comb my hair until every rib was in its proper place.

Down I came from the room with the accordion. My mother was sitting by the fire relaxing after the day's work.

'Where are you going, and why have you your Sunday clothes on?' she enquired.

'Oh, faith, I'm going playing,' I replied.

'They must be very hard up for a musician to say they got you. Off you go quickly now before your father sees you with your hair plastered with hair oil.'

I went to the door and stuck my head out into the open doorway.

'Listen, Mam,' I said, 'I'm taking your bicycle because there's a basket on the front of it.'

I tied the accordion in the basket with fishing cord and put a jute bag down on it. I was afraid to meet anybody at this time of evening, because, if I did, it is certain that they would spend the week talking about me.

When I got to the hall there was noise and giggling and talking outside the door. It was mostly the girls that were to be heard. 'A gaggle of women or a gaggle of geese', my father always said. In I went and walked up by the side of the hall. There was great clapping when they saw that I was carrying an accordion. I jumped up on the stage and placed a chair for myself in the centre. I had to pretend that I knew what I was doing. I took off my jacket and put it across the back of the chair. I sat down nice and easy and got my accordion ready. With that, a teacher stood up and said: 'The music is ready now so we'll have the first dance – "The Walls of Limerick".'

I had a great view from the stage because down the left-hand side of the hall to the front door there were at least one hundred and fifty of the finest girls I ever saw. Some red-haired, more of them fair, and more again with jet-black hair. Don't be talking about figures! Over at the other side of the hall were the boys, but they were the least of my worries.

I started playing and it wasn't long before the dance floor was full. 'Yes!' I said to myself, 'my music is going down well. I might as well cast an eye around and examine the fine sight here before me.' Upon my soul but it didn't take some of the local boys long to go hunting. That is when I knew I was in a fix. How would I meet any girl while I was up on the stage playing? I was throwing an eye at a couple of girls who were dancing near the stage. If you saw the wicked eye I got back from one of them. She'd kick the cart if a man went within twenty yards of her.

By God, but I was covered in sweat. I took a short break and then the teacher asked the students to do an old-time waltz. The local boys were welcome to dance with them he said. There was no need for the invitation because no sooner was the dance announced than the local boys made their way across the hall to the girls who were on the course. I noticed that there were more girls than boys doing that course and I was saying to myself that I would get my chance, too, before the night was over.

I was playing the second tune for the waltz when I noticed two girls in a corner by the stage. I noticed that one of them was giving me the eye now and then. She had a nice, kind face, a blue dress and a fine head of hair tumbling down her back. She was just like a girl should be. What was going through my head was how was I going to make contact with her.

'Put your two eyes back in your head and finish the waltz.'

It was the teacher who spoke from the bottom of the stage. He noticed that my music was going slightly astray with my staring at that girl. 'The Bridge of Athlone' was the dance that followed the waltz. The two girls were dancing right in front of me.

'You were looking at Eileen,' said one.

'I was,' I replied, 'and, if I was, she was looking at me too.' I was playing again and I suppose I was going well astray with the tune.

'Is-is-is there any chance of a date with her?'

'There's every chance,' she laughed.

I put my back into the music again and, after a while, the dance was over. Everybody sat down and the two girls sat at the bottom of the stage. The other girl went talking with a friend and shortly I got the glad eye from the girl I was interested in. My heart rose. I had got my cow across the river without even moving from the stage.

I noticed, too, that some of the local boys hadn't fared too well because they were on the floor for every dance with a different girl every time. Below me I saw my old friend, Seán Mór Ó Domhnaill. He was a handsome boy with black, wavy hair and the gift of the gab. But I wasn't too happy when I saw who he was talking to. Yes, indeed! The girl I hoped to date. By the way his head was moving, it was obvious that he was trying his best to get off with her. Oh, I thought, was Ireland not wide enough for him? He passed the bottom of the stage throwing shapes. There is no doubt that he was as good a dancer as was around at the time. He looked up at me and you'd think he knew what was going through my head. But she cast her eye in my direction and I knew then that everything was all right. When Seán Mór turned his head towards me there was a smile on his face; he knew the score. I suppose he had got his walking papers. He shook his fist at me, pretending to be angry.

After I had played the national anthem, the teacher shouted from the middle of the hall.

'There's a big céilí on tomorrow night until midnight. Now every student must go to their houses. The teachers will call the roll in every house between half past ten and eleven o'clock.' I was going out the door as fast as I could. Who should be outside the door but Seán Mór with a fine, tall, stout girl he had captured. He came over to me.

'I always said that you have the honey eye of a musician,' he began.

'What do you mean?' I replied.

Seán answered me: 'Tell me how you squared the Limerick girl without moving from the stage.'

'That's for me to know and you to find out,' I rejoined. I put my hand around my girl who was waiting patiently for me even though she didn't even know my name as yet. We walked a little way.

'Mike O'Shea is my name,' I told her. 'What's yours?'

'Eileen O'Sullivan from Limerick City. I'm afraid I haven't much Irish.'

'Your Irish will be as good as mine before the end of the course,' I assured her.

I was guiding her up Cáit Sayers' boreen by this time.

'You know,' she said, 'that I have to be back at the house by half past ten.'

Cáit Sayers' boreen was like O'Connell Street with all the courting couples. You would need a ticket to get a space by the ditch.

'Let's get out of here,' I said. 'I know a few more places.'

We went up Cliathán an Chaoil to another little road. It was a short cut between Muiríoch and Ballydavid and it was called Bhóithrín na nGéanna. Nobody would travel it by night as it was too lonely.

'Where are you staying, Eileen?' I asked her.

'Oh, in the big house at the end of the village.'

I wanted to put her mind at ease.

'The teachers call the roll in Cuimín and Bóthar Buí before they come to Muiríoch. It will be eleven o'clock before they call the roll in your house.'

'How do you know?' she asked me.

'Because it's the same teachers on the course this year as were on it last year and that's how they did it last year,' I assured her.

We were walking up the boreen. There were a few couples courting here and there. When we came to a nice, comfortable place we stopped and were just about to settle when we heard a voice from behind the ditch.

'Behave yourself or I'll tell the teacher.'

Eileen and I started to laugh.

'There's some poor girl in trouble,' she said.

'We'll move on another bit,' I replied. We came to a fine, comfortable spot a couple of yards from that place and we'll leave it at that because maybe you're getting too inquisitive. Upon my soul, I had her back in her house in time. Standing at the gate of the house were some of the boys and girls, not to mention the local 'dogs'.

'There's a big céilí tomorrow night,' said Eileen, pressing her hand in mine.

'Oh, I'll be there,' I promised.

When I had walked her to the door and said goodbye, I went back the road to John Mhicil's cabin where I had hidden my bicycle. I took the road north to Moorestown with my head in a spin from the events of the night. The luck I had to have secured Eileen before Casanova na Cille came her way!

The following evening my father was eating his supper at the top of the table. I had a basin of water at the bottom of the table; I was stripped to the waist and if I wasn't making use of the soap it isn't day yet.

'Where are you going tonight?' enquired Dainín, his mouth full of fresh mackerel.

'Oh, I'm playing without a doubt,' I replied.

'Oh, my soul to the devil … Tonight again? The youth have gone from the grace of God entirely,' Dainín snorted. I couldn't tell him that I was going to the céilí without having some excuse.

'Oh, 'twill take your mother an hour to get you out of bed again tomorrow morning. Are you going to spend the rest of your life travelling from place to place like Raftery?' he asked me. By God, but I couldn't let that one go past me.

'I'm getting paid for my music, whereas Raftery was playing for empty pockets. That's what he said in his poetry anyway,' I trumped him.

He pulled his chair a little way back from the table.

'You'd better jump out of bed the first time you're called to-morrow morning,' he warned me. 'We're going to Cill Chuáin thinning turnips. We don't want any night-walkers or morning sleepy-heads in this house.'

He had that fit put over him. I put on my new clothes without delay and hopped on my bicycle. It would be better for me to move away from the house quickly in case I'd say something that I would regret.

A lot of the local boys had gathered around the door of the hall. Some of them without the price of the céilí, more of them impatient to get in. I heard a whistle from the corner of the gable. It was Seán Mór who was there. We walked around to the side of the hall. He took a tie out of his pocket.

'Come here,' says he, 'put a knot in that for me.'

'Why didn't you put on the tie at home where you'd have a mirror?' I asked him.

He looked at me. 'To put a tie on me at home and to go through the parish this fine summer's evening … Christ, wouldn't John Aindí make a show of me if he saw me,' he replied.

When I was squeezing the knot under his jaw, I gave it a good pull.

'Listen,' I said to him, 'keep away from Eileen, I'll be keeping my eye on you.'

His face lit up with roguery.

'I have my own boat, Mike Daneen boy. And keep out of John Mhicil's cabin loft tonight because 'twill be in use!'

'Come on, we'd better go in. The band are starting up,' I said.

I didn't have to play on this night because it was a big céilí and I could spend the evening dancing as I pleased. I threw my eye around from the mouth of the door. Yes indeed, Eileen and her friend were sitting up near the shop.

'My girl is up there,' said Seán, facing up the side of the hall. The band started playing a nice, smooth waltz and a gang of us went out dancing. This was the first dance I ever had with Eileen.

After a couple of dances, I had to take off my jacket because there was a stream of sweat running down my backbone. After every dance, the girls would go back to their own side of the hall for fear the teacher would notice them talking to the boys. I was sitting beside Seán Mór.

'By the devil,' he said, 'isn't it hot?'

'Why wouldn't it be?' I replied, pointing my finger at the jacket he still had on.

'Oh that's a long story,' he told me, 'but that jacket will have to stay hanging from my bones tonight in any case. Come on up to the toilet and I'll tell you my story.'

We walked up to the toilet. When we got inside the door, Seán rose up the tail of his coat. All the back of his shirt was missing inside his coat. I began to laugh.

'Oh, in the name of God,' I chuckled, 'where's the rest of it?'

''Tis no laughing matter,' he retorted. 'This is the only white shirt I have in the world. I washed it today and put it on a bush behind the house to dry. A hoor of a calf came over the ditch and, whatever green grass was growing in the garden, didn't she start eating my shirt. I got a spade that was standing in a corner of the garden and I can tell you that she had the itch on the way home. If I was a minute later, I wouldn't have even the collar to put on myself. I suppose I have a dozen pins keeping it together on my back. Now do you understand my predicament?'

I spent the entire month with Eileen and, to tell the truth, we were getting very fond of each other. Every night after the céilí we would walk the roads somewhere. I suppose every boy in the place had a girl or, as one person quipped, there's no end to the supply.

The last evening of the course came and even though there were two other courses yet to come we had got to know the boys and girls on this course well and we were lonely at the thoughts of parting from them. On this last night, it was a little céilí that was held because the scholars had to be up early the following morning for the buses that would take them home. I spent the evening playing and, because of that, I had no dance with Eileen. But we had arranged to meet outside the hall. Would you believe, a fit of loneliness came over me and I don't think I was alone in that because when I cast my eye around the hall, it seemed to me that there was a gloomy appearance on them all, boys and girls. A couple of dances before the end of the céilí, the hall was half empty. That didn't surprise me in the least because it was the last night and the teachers bent the rules a little on the last night. I had to continue playing and I wasn't too thankful. I gave the odd look at Eileen sitting on a stool at the bottom of the stage. Would they ever call the last dance?

'Yes,' I said in my own mind, 'if a waltz is called for the last dance, and usually it is, 'twill be well shortened.'

No sooner had I played the national anthem than I gave a bucklep off the stage. I put my accordion in a safe place as I always did and headed for the door. She was waiting for me at the corner of the hall. We walked up the same road we walked on the first night we met. There wasn't a word out of either of us, only our two hands wound tightly around each other, her head on my right shoulder. Well, if tomorrow was the end of the world things couldn't be worse, I thought.

'Oh yes, Mike Daneen,' I thought, 'you spent the whole month with the one girl. Along with that you have grown fond of her and she'll be going away from you tomorrow and you'll have nothing as a result but loneliness and heartbreak. The devil mend you, 'twas easy to see you'd do something funny.'

Those are the thoughts that were going through my head while we walked down the boreen. Eileen was as miserable as I was, with not a word out of her only the odd bout of crying every now and then. After a while she got her talk.

'Will you write to me?' she implored.

What could I say but that I would. She put a piece of paper into my pocket.

'My address is written on that,' she said.

Oh mother of God, if there was a big céilí on itself we would have more time together.

'Listen, Eileen,' I said, 'where in your house is your room?' By God, but my mind was beginning to work again.

'At the south gable,' she told me, 'upstairs.' I was thinking for a while.

'Is there a window in the gable?' I asked her.

She looked at me between the two eyes. 'What's going on in your head?' she asked me.

I didn't say a thing for a while. Then I put it to her: 'Would you be afraid to climb down a ladder later in the night?'

'Why?' she replied, with the wonder of the world on her.

'I have a plan,' I told her. 'When the roll is called and the teachers are gone home, I'll get the ladder that's standing against John Aindí's cock of hay. I'll put it up to the window. I'll climb up and knock on it. Then open the window and I'll help you climb down the ladder. Close the window after you in case they find a breeze in the room. We'll hide the ladder then and it'll be up to us to decide when we part. What do you think of that for a plan?'

'Oh my God, I don't know,' she replied. 'What will we do if we're caught?' I pressed her to me.

'There's no fear,' I reassured her, 'and if we are caught itself, aren't you going home tomorrow?'

'I suppose you're right, my love,' she said. Then we headed for her house.

The local boys had gathered around the gate. Yes, there was no sign of any teacher yet. Eileen and I were a long time sitting there on the ditch across the road. There were four or five other boys loafing around on bicycles. After a while we noticed the front door of the house being opened. It was the woman of the house who was at the door.

'Are the blackguards from the parish of Moore gone home yet? Go home now because the girls are getting up early tomorrow morning,' she said.

'Thanks be to God,' I said to myself.

But the other cowboys weren't budging. I pretended to say goodbye to Eileen and she went into the house. Soon we saw the lights of a car coming from Ard na Carraige.

''Tis better for us to escape down the road,' said one boy. 'They're the teachers coming upon us and if they see any of us around here, they'll keep an eye on this house.'

We scattered down the road in the direction of the square in Muiríoch. We were talking, trying to waste time for a while.

'I wonder will the girls come out again?' ventured one fellow.

'Oh,' said I, 'as soon as the teachers are gone out the door, the woman of the house will bolt it.'

The car full of teachers passed through the village. 'May the road rise with them,' said Éamonn Ó Dálaigh. 'Are you going home?' he asked me, noticing that I had no bicycle. 'If you have no bicycle, hop up on the bar of mine,' he said.

'Oh,' I told him, 'I have it in John Aindí's haggard. Listen to me, stay around for a while.' His face had a puzzled look. 'I'll need help with the ladder,' I informed him.

There was no need to say any more. He laughed and shook his head.

'Hide your bicycle and we'll slip away from this gang,' I whispered, pulling at the sleeve of his jacket.

'Right, Mike Daneen,' he said out loud, 'jump up on the bar and we'll head for home.'

He said this so that the other boys wouldn't have any idea of what we were planning. I jumped up and off we went through Muiríoch until we reached John Aindí's cabin. He caught his bicycle and put it behind the ditch in one go.

'Where is the ladder?' he asked me as he jumped the ditch.

'It's up against the cock of hay,' I told him.

We took the ladder, one of us at each end. We stole up by the stream and into the haggard at the back of Eileen's house.

'Watch out,' I warned, 'there's a dyke near the ditch.'

'I suppose you have every foot of this haggard walked by now,' he said to me. 'Where do you want the ladder?' he asked me, standing there at the back of the house. 'The gable window. And when you have it standing at the window, you can head for home,' I told him.

'Oh, I see. Go home when you have the ladder brought here,' he said.

'Do you know any of the girls in this house?' I asked him.

'Any one of them will do me, they're all the same,' he said.

I climbed the ladder nice and easy for fear that any of the rungs would be rotten. Éamonn was at the bottom of the ladder with his foot against it in case it would slip.

I knocked lightly on the window, but, if I did, there was no sound from the room. Then I knocked on the pane with a penny I took from my pocket. The window opened. It was Eileen's friend who was there.

'She'll be with you in a minute,' she told me.

'Listen,' I said, 'I have another boy with me. Maybe you could come out as well.' She opened the window a little wider and put her head out.

'Where is he?' she asked.

'He's at the bottom of the ladder,' I informed her.

'I can't see him,' she said, 'the night is too dark. Is he good looking?'

'Did you ever see a picture of Rock Hudson?' I asked her. 'Well, he wouldn't hold a candle to the man at the bottom of the ladder.'

She ran to the back of the room to get her jacket. 'I'll be with you… I'll be with you,' she cried.

Eileen came to the window, dressed for the road.

'Turn around and come down backwards,' I advised her. 'I'll take hold of your leg and I'll guide it on the rungs of the ladder.'

She was shaking with fear. 'Do you know,' she said as she put her leg out of the window, 'we're sure to be caught.'

'Be quiet, girl, and have sense for yourself,' I told her.

While all this was going on, the boys who were in the square in Muiríoch were going by on their bicycles with every shout coming from them.

They stopped directly in front of the house.

'Oh,' said one, 'Isn't it a funny time of the night for two carpenters to be putting in a window.'

The others started to laugh. The door of the house opened.

'Oh,' said Eileen, 'we're done for,' pulling herself back inside the window.

'Go home, you pack of blackguards,' said the woman.

Yes indeed! Everything was in a right mess. I looked down at the bottom of the ladder, but Éamonn had scampered over the ditch. A good run is better than a bad stand I said to myself, climbing down the ladder. I was halfway down when the woman turned the corner of the house with a brush in her hand. I jumped from the fourth rung and, if I did, she went for me with the brush and hit me between my shoulder blades. Before she readied herself for the second attack, I had taken my legs over the ditch.

'Take that, you little tailor of the women. Think of the cheek to get a ladder and be climbing into a private room. Off with you now to wherever you came from and don't come back. This is no kip shop.'

Oh, Blessed Mother, the pain that was in my back. I thought it was broken in two halves. I escaped as quickly as I could with my shoulders hunched and I made out the place where my bicycle was. Éamonn was there before me, his mouth wide open, laughing at the wretch in front of him with his back bent to the ground.

'This is no cause for mocking,' I said, trying to get my bicycle from inside the ditch. I wasn't doing too well and Éamonn had to help me. When I had got my bicycle I spent half an hour there without moving. I recovered from the pain after a while.

'Come on,' I said to Éamonn, throwing my leg over the saddle as I hit the road. Éamonn followed me.

'Oh,' he joked, 'are we going back to that house again?'

'If Elizabeth Taylor was waiting there for me, I wouldn't go within an ass's roar of it,' I assured him.

9

After the students had left, the place got very quiet and settled. Only the odd visitor came around, even though the weather couldn't have been better. I was waiting for the results of the exam I did in the Tech and, when they came out, I discovered that I had passed every subject, a thing that lifted my heart greatly. Then I began to think that I should go and look for a permanent job.

Things would be bad enough trying to pass the long winter nights without being stuck by the fire in the daytime too. I tried every tradesman in the locality hoping that some one of them would want an apprentice. But, unfortunately, it was the same answer I got from them all: they hadn't enough work themselves to keep going.

August had come and the farmers were finishing the harvest. I'd get downhearted when I'd think of the long winter before me with no hope of earning a penny and I still too young to sign for the dole.

I was binding oats up in Cill Chuáin Uachtair. Or should I say that I was binding oats and thistles! At the very most, I had a week's work with this farmer without any hope of work until the following spring again. There were three of us working in the field; one gathering the oats and two binding. You'd think from the way the other two were handling the oats that there were no thistles in them. It must have been that the skin on their hands was as tough as an ass's skin. The field was about five acres in size and it took us the most of a fortnight to cut, gather and bind it. When the last stook was put standing in that field, I almost shouted with joy.

'I can tell you,' I said to my two companions, 'the next autumn won't find me in a field of thistles in Cill Chuáin or in any other village around here either.'

By this time there were a thousand thistle thorns in my skin. The two had their mouths open laughing at me. I left them there and headed for home with my two hands swollen from the thorns. I washed and scraped myself as well as I could. Then I got a basin of hot water and poured a drop of Dettol into it. I scalded my hands as I was afraid they would get infected from the thorns.

When I was dressed and clean, I jumped on my bicycle and headed for the town of Dingle. I told my mother that I was going to the pictures. But it wasn't the pictures I was thinking about that night. Not likely. The director of the summer courses lived there and I hadn't been paid a penny for playing for them all summer.

It wasn't long before I was in the town of Dingle. I stopped in Green Street outside the house where the director was staying. I knocked fine and handy on the door, but there was no movement from within. I knocked harder. The woman of the house came to open it.

'There's a bell on the side of the door,' she barked. 'All you have to do is press it. There's no need to break the door.'

I didn't say a word, though you can imagine what came to the tip of my tongue.

'Is Tomás inside?' I enquired. The door was open by only half a foot. You'd think I had some disease.

'He hasn't finished his tea yet,' was the reply.

Oh, that was life in those times. The slave had to wait at the door while the gentleman filled his belly. She shut the door and left me to wait. I rested my shoulder against the frame of the door. It is best for a person to have patience.

After a while the door opened and the teacher came out. He was wiping his puss with some kind of white paper.

'Well,' I said, 'did it come?'

'What do you mean?' he replied.

'The money I earned hard playing for the courses all summer long.'

'Oh,' he said, 'I was going to have a word with you on the last night of the course, but you were gone home too quickly.' Yes, I said to myself. It has come.

'I'm here now,' I told him. 'It's as good a time as any to give it to me.'

'Well, I sent an account to the Department of Education concerning the total costs of running the course, and your expenses among them. In the letter of reply, it was pointed out to me that there was something amiss.'

'But was there any money in the letter?' I persisted.

'Take it easy until I tell you. As I said to you, I requested the costs of the music separately. The answer I received was that every other course was using records for dance music and, in consequence, the department would not make money available to pay musicians any more.'

Oh boy, the blood ran up to my skull.

'What the hell are you saying?' I demanded. I shoved the door in.

'Take it easy now, my good man,' he warned me. 'I have no cure for it.'

I shoved my nose as close to his face as I could.

'Was it you who made the bargain with me?' I asked him.

'Well, yes,' he replied, 'but I had no knowledge of the cutbacks in the department.'

I was boiling with rage by this time.

'I'll bet you didn't cut back on your own wages,' I told him.

'Take it easy,' he repeated. I had the head lost by now.

'You tinker without a conscience,' I began, 'I'd swear you got the money and put it in your own pocket.'

He retreated and attempted to shut the door but I had my shoe between it and the threshold.

'Away with you now, my good man, or I'll summon the police,' he said.

I suppose I had recovered some of my senses by this time because I said to myself that peace was better than war. I backed out the door and it was closed behind me. What was I to do? I had no proof that I had made any bargain after all I had sweated on the stage. I headed down the street like a dog with his tail between his legs. What could I do now? I'd be stuck in this place and not a day's work to be had. Yerra, as I was in Dingle I said to myself that I'd go to the pictures. I went as far as Katie Sarah's window because it was there the posters advertising the pictures were displayed. A western was showing that night and I loved those same westerns. Maybe 'twould rise my spirits to go to the pictures.

It was two shillings for the soft seats and one shilling for the others. There was better *craic* in the cheaper seats. The 'Pathé News' was on when I came to my seat. News from every part of the world. When the lights came up before the big picture started, I found that an old friend of mine was sitting beside me.

'Oh, is it yourself that's there, Muiris?' I began. I told him the tale of the goings-on of the evening.

'In the name of God,' he said, 'if anybody ever earned that money, it was yourself after all you sweated playing alone on that stage with no help from anyone.'

'Yerra,' I confided in him, 'that's not the worst part of the story. I was going to go to Dublin next Saturday for the All-Ireland football semi-final and I was going to take the boat to England on Sunday evening.'

'England!' exclaimed Muiris, with two wide eyes on him. 'And you only sixteen years of age. You'll only get a boy's wages.'

'Anything would be better than going from post to pillar around here without even the price of a box of matches in my pocket,' I replied. He looked at me.

'I always thought you were cracked in the head,' he said, 'but now I think you're clean out of your mind.'

I lit a cigarette and the conversation didn't proceed any farther because the picture started. To tell the truth, my mind wasn't on the film. Forty things were running through my head. The film finished around half past eleven. As we went out the door, Muiris asked me where I had left my bicycle.

'Back in a derelict building in Clery's haggard,' I informed him. Muiris told me that his bicycle was in the same place.

'If you left your bicycle on the side of the street,' he said, ''twould be lifted by some bosthoon and gone out Goat Street with a good chance that you'd never again see it.' We didn't say another word for a while.

'But are you in earnest about England?' he asked me.

We were walking by the police barracks by this time. As surely as if he was Dainín, he stopped in the middle of the street and looked me between the eyes.

'Did you draw this down at home?' he demanded. I put my hand on his shoulder.

'Do you think I'm a pure eejit?' I replied. 'If the old fellow or the old lady knew what was in my head, they'd go crazy. What I was going to say to them was that I was going to the match and that I would spend a week in Dublin with a cousin of mine. When my letter would arrive from London, I'd be far away and maybe with a job. What could they do then? But don't even mention it now because everything is in a mess when I don't have the money for the road.'

We were making our way down towards the pier by this time. It was a fine, soft autumn night with the moon full above us.

'Listen, Mike,' Muiris said, 'your luck is in. If you had the money for the road, would you have it paid back before Christmas?' I was doubtful about what was in his head.

'I'm not going to take any money from you because you have enough responsibilities of your own,' I told him.

'Now Mike,' he continued, 'I don't smoke and I don't drink a pint. The only time of the year I need money is at Christmas. Now, I'm going to give you thirty pounds that I have up on top of the cupboard at home. You'll get it on two conditions …'

It was hard to refuse such an offer. 'Go on,' I said.

'Don't ever tell your family who gave you the money for the road,' he warned me, 'and, number two, try to have it paid back before Christmas.' I put my hand around his shoulder.

'My dear friend,' I said, 'you have my word, and I'll never forget you.' There wasn't a word from either of us for a while.

'Oh Christ,' he exclaimed, 'if Dainín ever finds out that I gave you money, he'll throw me into a boghole.'

The two of us burst out laughing.

It was midnight and half an hour with it when we arrived at his house. We went into the kitchen as quietly as we could so as not to wake the household. He started searching on top of a cupboard that was in the corner near the hob. After a while, he took down a fistful of notes that were folded and tied with cord.

''Tis no wonder that you have no desire to leave,' I said, getting the fill of my eyes from the bundle of notes. 'If I had a pile of money like that, I wouldn't leave this place either,' I told him.

'Farming is getting better these past few years,' he replied, 'and my family want to keep me at home. They give me plenty of money and they'll leave me the farm when I'm twenty-one.' With that, he counted out the money.

'Go now,' he said, 'and may every good luck go with you.'

'Yes,' I said, 'I'd better go to see if I can get any wink of sleep. But I promise you one thing, and that is that you'll have your money back before Christmas comes upon you.' He gave me a lonesome look.

'I suppose,' he said, 'you'll settle down over in England for the rest of your life.'

'I'm going to spend one year in England,' I told him, 'and then I'll have the price of going to America. Maybe I'll spend a number of years there. By that time, things will surely have improved in our own little country. If I can at all, I'll die in Ireland.'

Yes, I said goodbye and went off on my bicycle. I felt a catch in my heart as I neared our old homestead.

The Saturday morning before the semi-final, I got out of bed early. I wasn't able to get a wink of sleep there were so many things going through my head. There was fog right down to the mouth of the door giving a dirty, gloomy appearance to the place. I put on my Sunday clothes and my new shoes. I got a small suitcase that was shoved under the bed. I threw a couple of old shirts into it and a couple of trousers and an old pair of hobnailed boots that I used when I was cutting turf with a *sleán*. I shoved it under the bed again so that I could face the kitchen. My father was sitting at the head of the table, drinking tea. My mother was making a cake of bread down at the bottom of the table.

'Oh, God help us, he's up,' joked my father. 'Are you going to work in some office?' he continued. I sat down, pulled a mug towards me and poured tea into it.

'I'll tell you where I'm going,' I replied, 'I'm going as far as Dublin to the All-Ireland football semi-final between Kerry and Derry.' The two looked at each other.

'And have you enough money for the road?' they enquired.

'I have, faith,' I said, 'I got the money for playing at the courses last night.' My father got his cap that was hanging inside the door.

'Oh,' he said, 'if you have your own money, away with you.'

'I suppose you'll be home again on Sunday evening,' said my mother.

'Yerra,' I told her, 'I'll give a week there. I'll stay with the O'Haras.'

Nobody went against me as they were related to us. I finished my breakfast quickly. My father got his coat and walked towards the door.

'If you ask me,' he exclaimed, 'the young lads of today are full of *teaspach*. Not only that but they're gone mad altogether.' He was giving another sermon. 'When I was young …' He was still talking as he was going out the door. I gave a good, long look at him out through the window until he disappeared from sight wherever he was going.

I went up to the room to get my little suitcase.

'Is that all you're going to eat or why haven't you eaten your boiled egg? You have a long journey ahead of you.' It was my mother who spoke.

'You don't know the half of it,' I said to myself. 'I'll take your bicycle,' I told her. 'Somebody will go to collect it in Clery's haggard.' I got the bicycle and fixed the suitcase behind it. My mother followed me out to the gate.

'Take care of yourself in Dublin,' she pleaded. 'There's every kind of a tinker there.' I said goodbye to her and went down the road. When I had gone some distance, I turned back and saw that she was still at the gate looking after me. You'd think she knew that she wouldn't see me for a long time. With that, a catch came to my throat and I found it hard to keep the tears from falling.

While I was cycling up Mám A' Lochaigh, I looked down at the Parish of Moore and, looking down, my tears fell in plenty. There before me were Béal A' Chuain, Baile Dháith Tower, Baile Reo, the bottom of Mount Brandon and all the places that I knew so well. 'Yes,' I said to myself, 'I'll be back to you and my pockets won't be empty.' I got the half past ten bus from Dingle to Tralee. The Dublin train wasn't leaving until one o'clock. That gave me a chance to have a bite to eat and a cup of tea in Tralee. About ten to one, I got to the station and there was a big crowd gathered there before me. I went up to the ticket office to buy a ticket for the journey that was in front of me. I told my story to the girl who was selling the tickets. I'd be in Dublin tonight, I told her, and I'd be heading for England the following morning.

'It's all the one,' she reassured me, 'this ticket is valid for a fortnight.' She asked me what part of England I was going to.

'London,' I replied cockily.

'That'll be seventeen pounds and sixpence,' she informed me. The ticket was cheaper than I thought it would be. This was my first journey on a train even though I was sixteen years of age. I boarded the train and sat near a window so that I could see all around me.

The train pulled out from the station after a while. The farther it got from the big town, the faster it went. The biggest wonder to me was how it kept between the narrow rails when it was travelling so fast and how it didn't slip off of them and land in the middle of some field or other. The person who thought it up had some head. Before long we were in Rathmore, our last stop in Co. Kerry. It was then the thoughts started going through my head. Yes, I was after leaving home on my way to England to look for work. Wasn't it the wretched little place where I was born? The fathers and mothers of Ireland rearing their families and, when they're reared, they emigrate and leave their parents alone and lonely at the end of their lives. I wonder if it's the people themselves who are to blame. Wasn't it lucky I told my mother I'd be in Dublin for a week. If I hadn't said that much, the guards would be looking for me by Tuesday, I suppose. My mother would be fretful when any one of us was away from home. Many thoughts like that ran through my head on the journey. We left Mallow behind us. What would my brother Dónall say when I walked in to him on Monday morning? He was in London for a number of years. I suppose it would be the War of the Two Kings between us.

A man who was sitting beside me gave me an address in Dublin where I could stay. According to him, this place was only an ass's roar from Croke Park. The train pulled into Dublin about six o'clock. When I got out of it, I stopped for a while to look around. I walked slowly out of the station. It was a fine sight I looked upon outside. Big, tall buildings on every side of me. Thousands of people around me and they all in a hurry. Ah, I thought, isn't this a very busy place.

'Hello sir!' I saluted some person who was going past me. But, boy! All I got by way of a salutation from him was a peevish look.

I met a policeman on the bridge outside the station. I gave him the piece of paper I had with the address of the lodging house on it. He gave me good directions and it wasn't long before I arrived at my destination. It was belonging to a man from Caherciveen and he called it 'The Castle'. I've stayed there many times since.

I was up early on Sunday morning. I wasn't used to traffic or noise or sleeping in a strange place. I made out the dining room and I can tell you that I got the fine smell of fried meat when I was coming down the stairs. A plate was put before me that morning with food on it fit for the king of Spain. Fried bacon, white and black pudding and a fried egg as well.

After I had filled my belly, I thanked the people of the house, paid for my bed and board and headed for Croke Park. There was a while to go before the minor match. I never saw the likes of the crowd that was on the street and they all making for Croke Park. Some of them with the Kerry colours, more with the Derry colours.

It was easy to get a seat in the Hogan Stand that day. It was hot enough between the two teams for the first twenty minutes and there was a tremendous contest between Mick O'Connell and Jim McKeever at midfield. Yes indeed, there were a couple of old warriors on the Kerry team who should have been sitting with the spectators. They were much too slow and they had their best years given. It was obvious in the second half that there was no way back for Kerry and Derry were getting the upper hand at their ease. Even though Mick O'Connell was sending in plenty of ball to the forwards, they hadn't the legs to get away from the Derry backs. Derry won easily. I was fed up leaving Croke Park, but what was to be done? I said we'd have another day.

10

At nine o'clock that night the mail boat sailed from Dún Laoghaire. Boy, if you saw the size of that boat! She was as wide as the main street in Dingle and if she was one foot, she was three hundred, or so it seemed to me. I was amazed as to how anything as big or as heavy in the water as that could float. You'd think that the whole population of Ireland were abandoning their native place, there was such a crowd on the boat that night. I asked one of the crew was there as big a crowd on the boat every night.

'It's always like this in summer,' he told me.

'Oh, God help us! There won't be a soul left in Ireland if this keeps up,' I said to myself.

There were people everywhere; they were on deck and below deck. If a person wanted a bunk, it could be had for an extra pound, but somebody told me it wasn't worth getting one. When she had cleared the harbour, there was a huge crowd on deck all looking back towards Howth and the other bit of Ireland that was in front of them and slipping away in the darkness. There were people there with handkerchiefs to their eyes and they making great cries.

'Oh,' I said to myself, 'didn't the Man Above give us a great cross that we can't earn a living in our own place.'

A load of sadness came upon my own heart. I walked around the boat to put the fit of loneliness from me and went down the stairs. There were tea and sandwiches to be had down there and other drinks if you were thirsty. There was a man in a corner playing fine lively music. I found out afterwards that he was from some part of the county Galway and I can tell you he had music. There was a crowd gathered round him, many of them with big pints of porter, and they had all the appearances of not having a trouble in the world. They were drinking heavily and when they weren't drinking they were making every bucklep to the music. When the music man took a break, somebody would rise a verse of a song. I sat down at my ease and was enjoying the *craic*. There was a shortening of the road, or should I say the sea, about it. A number of songs were sung that wouldn't go down too well with the Queen of England if she was in the company! Some man said after a while that we were approaching the coast of Wales. The bar was closed and we were told to prepare ourselves to land. People were stretched asleep everywhere and more were doubled over the railings puking their guts up with seasickness. I'm afraid they hadn't their sea legs.

She pulled in to the pier and everybody was ordered to get ready for the customs. I wasn't going to delay the customs man with the few clothes I had in my suitcase. But God save us, there were some people there and you'd think they had the furniture and everything in the house with them. Holy Mary! What were all the clothes for?

After going through the customs, we boarded a train that was waiting for us. The train would take us directly into London without any more fooling around. I followed the crowd onto the train and got a seat for myself. I wasn't long in the seat when I fell fast asleep and I don't remember another thing until the conductor woke me. I asked him where we were and he told me that we were about an hour away from London. I went to the toilet and tidied myself up.

When I was looking out the window of the train, I noticed that the houses were getting more plentiful as time was going by and shortly all the houses were running into one another. Never in my life did I get a smell so horrible and so stale as when the train was coming into London city. I thought Dublin was bad when I was there the previous day, but the air was fine and wholesome there in comparison to this place. London is a big, long, wide city. I wasn't long finding that out when I went looking for my brother's flat. I had his address written on a piece of paper and he was living in a place called Woodgreen.

It was the tube, or underground train, that took me from the station, Paddington, to Woodgreen. They ran on electricity, that is the underground trains, and you'd travel from one end of the city to the other in them inside an hour. When I came out at Woodgreen station the streets were crowded and everybody was rushing madly, just like they were in Dublin. They were yellow and black and white – some of them as black as the three-legged pot we had at home. There were stout men and thin men there, young and old. Handsome women and women you could only compare to monkeys and they taking the legs from under each other wherever they were going. I looked up the street. I could see a cinema on the left with a clock placed cleverly on top. It was only half past ten in the morning. If I went to my brother's flat it is likely that he would be gone to work and I would have to explain my story to the woman of the house.

After enquiring and searching, I made out Victoria Road. I was looking for number thirty. I came to the door. Every house looked the same because each house, from one end of the street to the other, was made of red brick. I pressed the button that was on the frame of the door. After a while I saw a shadow through the glass coming towards me. Standing in front of me was a small, stout woman with a grey head on her and a big wide face.

'What do you want?' she asked me abruptly. I told her that I was a brother of Dónall O'Shea's.

'I suppose he's gone to work,' I said. She told me that he was, looking at me suspiciously.

'I find it strange that Dónall said nothing to me about you coming over,' she said. I told her that he wouldn't have any notion that I was coming.

'Come in,' she said after a while. We went in through a dark hall to the kitchen. She faced the stairs.

'Follow me,' she said.

From the appearance of the house, I'd say it was built for a couple of hundred years. She took me into a small room near the top of the stairs. There was a fireplace in the room and it looked like it didn't see a fire for many a day. I asked her how much I would have to pay for the room, casting my eye around at the same time. She said she wanted three pounds a week and that included breakfast in the morning and dinner in the evening as well. I put my hand in my pocket and gave her three pounds. I wonder if it was that her heart softened when she saw the money but she brought me down to the kitchen and made me a mug of tea and a sandwich. The bread was slightly stale, but who would complain? It was food.

The day was still young and, instead of listening to that old woman's nonsense, I said to myself that I'd better go out and look for work. I asked her where the most likely place would be to go looking. She wrote down the addresses of a couple of big factories. It wouldn't be much good looking for outside work at this time of year. I said goodbye to her and headed off down the street in the direction of Woodgreen. I went on the underground train then and asked the conductor about where was the best place to get off and he told me when I showed him my list that I'd be only a few hundred yards from the first factory if I got off at St Paul's Road.

After I got off the train, I headed for the first place that was on my list. But there was no work there.

'Come back next spring,' they said to me.

Upon my soul, but wasn't that a great help to Dainín's son! I gave the most of the day going from place to place like a tinker. I had a pain in my two legs from walking and my hopes were falling as the day was going by. I looked at a clock that was across the street from me. It was already half past four.

'I'll go back to my flat,' I said to myself, 'and I'll be fresher in the morning.'

I was just going to jump on a bus when I noticed this place down a backstreet. I decided that it wouldn't cost me a penny to try it and I went down to it. I went in through a door that was half open. The place wasn't as small as I thought at first. A middle-aged man approached me. He asked me if I was looking for somebody. I thought 'twould be no harm to do a bit of acting. I was expecting the same answer here as I got in twenty other places before this. I found it hard enough to understand him.

'Out with it, mate,' he said.

I looked him plaintively between the eyes. I asked him if he had any work for me. I told him that I had come across on the boat last night. He looked at me and questioned me about the kind of work I had done in Ireland. I told him the truth, that I cut turf in the bog, that I bound oats and so on. He was thinking for a while. That was no bad sign. He told me to look around the factory to see what kind of work the men were doing. He asked me could I read a blueprint. My heart rose because I had studied mechanical drawing in Dingle Tech. I told him that I had spent two years studying in the Tech. He took a big white paper out of his pocket and laid it on a table inside the door. He told me to look at the paper and we'd go up through the factory.

We walked through the middle of it until we came as far as three men who were putting different parts of a machine together. He opened the blueprint in front of me again. He pointed his finger at a part of the drawing. He asked me to tell him where that part was on the ground. Without delay, I picked up the part and told him that this was it. When he had been thinking for a while, he told me to come in at eight o'clock the following morning. I thanked him and shook his hand. My steps were light going towards the door. The fatigue left my bones and I was as happy as if I had won the Sweep.

When I was out in the street I wrote down the address of the place. You could say I had wings as I was going for the train. I felt so light. I was thinking what would my brother Dónall say now.

'Oh my lovely boy, isn't it me that's independent?' I said to myself.

I went on the train and was travelling for about ten minutes before I asked the conductor any question. I asked him was I far from Woodgreen. He told me that if I kept going in the direction I was travelling I'd be farther from it, because I was travelling in the wrong direction. He told me to get off at the next station and to go across the bridge. Oh, Holy Mary, excitement is no good in a strange place.

It was making for six o'clock when I arrived at my flat. My brother wasn't home yet.

'Yes,' I was thinking, 'there's nothing to stop me writing home tonight and putting a five pound note in the letter – that'll sweeten things.'

I was going working the following morning and I owed nothing to anybody. I wasn't depending on de Valera any more. The woman of the house asked me would I eat my dinner now or would I wait for my brother. I let her know that I'd wait for him. I stretched out on the bed and if anybody was ever exhausted, I was that evening. After a quarter of an hour I got up because if I spent another minute in bed I'd be asleep. I threw a few splashes of water on my face, combed my hair and headed for the kitchen. I wanted to be sitting there when Dónall came in to see the surprise on his face when he saw me there before him. The man of the house was sitting at the fire and I introduced myself. He was a small thin man who hadn't much talk, but he was getting great satisfaction from smoking tobacco. But the woman of the house had enough talk for the two of them. She was there setting the table and she complaining and grumbling about the neighbours. I heard the front door opening.

'Here he is for sure,' I said to myself. I heard the footsteps coming into the hall. The woman of the house was coming in from the back kitchen with a pot of potatoes.

'Hello,' said Dónall to her, standing in the doorway into the kitchen.

'Have you any "hello" for me, Dónall?' I asked him. The cap fell from his hand to the floor.

'Oh the devil! Mike. Are you alive or dead or am I seeing a ghost?' We held each other tightly. 'Where did you come from?' he asked me. 'Oh, Mother Mary, I didn't get such a fright since the day Tomáisín Sheáin Bheaglaoi's bull chased me long ago.'

I wasn't able to move for laughing.

'Yerra, the devil take you, why didn't you write?' he asked.

'If I did,' I replied, "twould be many a day and a night before you saw me.' He moved back from me.

'Don't tell me… You didn't tell them at home that you were coming, did you?'

I sat on the chair. 'I was up at the All-Ireland semi-final in Dublin and I said to myself that I'd take a trip over. They wouldn't be expecting me for a week anyway because I told them I'd stay a week in Dublin,' I told him.

He rubbed the palm of his hand to his forehead. 'Thanks be to the good God,' he said. 'You can write home tonight and tell them. Oh, in the name of God, they'll make ructions.'

The meal was ready and we sat down at the table.

'Yes,' said Dónall, 'we'll have to look for a job for you tomorrow.' I gave him a fine independent answer.

'There's no need,' I told him, 'because I have a job got already.' The piece of meat he had in his mouth almost choked him.

'My life on you,' he exclaimed, 'where did you get the job?'

'I have the address in my pocket,' I told him.

The woman of the house was there with her two eyes going out of her head trying to make out what we were up to. It wasn't long before she put in her four pence worth.

'Speak English, you are in England now,' she insisted.

If she did, Dónall answered her menacingly. He asked her was there a law in the country that said people had to speak English. He looked at me and continued in Irish.

'She's a nosey strap,' he said.

When we had eaten dinner, we went up to the room and Dónall gave me pen and paper.

'Write a few lines home in the name of God,' he urged me.

When I had the letter written I put a five pound note into it and addressed it.

'What did you think of the dinner?' Dónall asked me after a while, with a smile on his face.

'Oh wisha,' I said to him, 'it put me in mind of nothing but the swill we'd give to the pigs at home.'

'Mike boy,' Dónall continued, 'as soon as we can get a room some place, we'll show the soles of our feet to that bitch.'

'The sooner, the better,' I agreed, 'or we won't have a lung left between us.'

Dónall asked me was I questioned about my age in the place I got the job. I told him that no question like that was put to me. He gave a while thinking.

'Very good,' he said. 'I'll go to the Labour tomorrow and I'll get your cards for you. If anybody on the job asks you, say that you'll be nineteen on the second of February. That's your birthday, isn't it?'

He explained to me that if I let them know that I was under eighteen years of age, I'd only get a boy's wage.

'You'd better give Baile Ghainnín instead of Carrachán for your address,' he advised me, 'in case you have to escape to some other place.'

'Do they ever look for a birth certificate in the Labour?' I asked him. He laughed.

'Indeed they don't,' he told me. 'Come on down to Woodgreen and we'll put the letter in the post. I have stamps in the room.'

We walked down the street until we came to a pillar box. Never in all my life did I see a place so lit up. There were lights in places with no other function but to go out and come on.

'Holy Mary,' I exclaimed, 'some of those lights would be

badly wanted in the parish of Moore where they have only small oil lamps on the side of the walls. Sure half the parish is going blind from reading the Kerryman without proper light.'

Dónall was full of questions. How was this fellow? What killed the other fellow? I was in no humour for answering questions because I was tired in every bone in my body. We did nothing only to throw the letter into the box and return to our flat again.

'The woman of the house will wake us in the morning,' Dónall informed me when he was going into his own room.

I put out the light and, as soon as my head hit the pillow, I fell into a sound sleep.

11

'Breakfast ready for steady boarders!' I jumped up in the bed.

'Oh yes,' it dawned on me, 'I'm in London.'

I had a good stretch and put my two feet on the floor. I switched on the electric light so as to find my clothes. I pulled out the small suitcase I had shoved under the bed. I put on an old pants I had brought for work and put my old shoes near the leg of the bed.

I knocked on Dónall's door. 'Have you a razor?' I asked him.

''Tis in the bathroom, near the basin,' he told me.

I went into the bathroom and shaved and got myself ready. I'd have no business looking like a tinker on my first day at work.

When I came into the kitchen, Dónall was already sitting at the table. There was a twisted rasher and a fried egg on the plate the woman of the house had put in front of me and if there's any good in grease, my breakfast was swimming in it. But, upon my soul, I ate it – because it's better to have something in your stomach for the day's work than to be weak with the hunger.

'I'll be with you as far as Finnsbury Park on the train,' said Dónall, 'and two stops after that, you get off. Turn left when you come up from the underground. You'll only have a two minutes' walk then.'

I tied my bootlaces and we headed for the station. You should hear the noise the hobnailed boots made on the pavement! I nearly fell over backwards a few times because the hobnails were slipping on the pavement.

'You'll have to get a pair of working shoes with rubber soles as soon as you have the price of them,' Dónall advised me. 'Those hobnailed boots will put you on the flat of your back when the frosty weather comes,' he said.

I make out that everybody that passed me was looking back at me. One man gave a little laugh and said, 'Welcome to London, Pat.'

'What in the devil is wrong with him,' I asked Dónall, 'when Mike is my name?' Dónall started to laugh.

'Every Irishman is called "Pat" here, no matter what his right name is. That man is an Irishman and he knows well than no one would be wearing boots like them only a man straight over from Ireland.' That sort of got my temper up.

'Yerra, the devil sweep him. I suppose he was never down in a boghole,' I exploded.

I got to the factory at a quarter to eight; that was a quarter of an hour before work started there. I made the sign of the cross and faced into my first day working in a foreign country. I was standing impatiently in the doorway. Workers were coming thick and fast and they were putting cards into some machine. The man who met me the evening before came in with his coat under his arm. He beckoned to me with his hand. He brought me into an office and started to question me. He asked me to give him my name, my address and my date of birth. When I had given him that much, he told me to go down to George Houghton on the assembly line and say to him that I would be working with him. I went down through the factory and was shown where this George Houghton was working. He was a middle-aged man who was born and reared in London. He had more than twenty years given working for United Aircoil; that was the name of the factory. Even though he was from London, 'twas no bother to understand him. He was used to be dealing with people from various places. He told me to watch him and the two others who were working with him and to take in everything. He told me not to be afraid and that I would learn everything bit by bit, and, if I had any question, not to be backward in asking. When he found out that I could follow a blueprint, he was delighted. He pointed to two who were near us and said you couldn't turn your back on them or they would have some part turned upside down.

I found it very difficult to understand what those two said, but I got used to hearing one particular word they used very often. I can tell you that it wasn't used in our house back at home, because an ounce of soap would be put in the mouth of anyone who used it there. I also got used to hearing every Irishman called 'Pat' by the English. George gave me every help and you would know that he had gone through life and had understanding for people.

A little bell sounded at the top of the factory. A man opened a window.

'Tea up!' he shouted.

Every machine in the place stopped and everybody went in the direction of the canteen that was open for tea. Two pence it cost and it was well worth it. There was a man sitting beside me while I was drinking my drop of tea. He was talking to a man who was opposite him. 'Upon my life but you're an Irishman,' I said in my own mind. It was mainly Englishmen who were working with me and the biggest fault I had to find with them was that they couldn't put two words together without using that ugly word I mentioned before. I picked up courage after a while and spoke to the man who was near me. I asked him was he from Ireland. He was from Dublin city he told me; Ken Fitzpatrick was his name. He thought at first that I was from Cork. I let him know that I was a Kerryman. He caught me by the hand and told me that he was working on the assembly line and that I could come to him if anything was puzzling me. Well, now there was a man from my own country near me, thanks be to God. The bell rang again and it was time to go back to work. When I was walking back I said to Ken in a whisper that I thought the English were very fond of birds. He burst out laughing. He told me that the birds they were talking about were birds without feathers or wings. Oh boy! Wasn't I green. Of course, it's women they were talking about, Ken told me, and, if I'd like to meet him at lunchtime, he'd give me a few more little tips like that. I promised to meet him. When he was walking away from me, he was still talking: 'Sex is the religion in this country, my boy,' he informed me. I spent lunchtime in his company that day because I had a lot of questions to put to him. I asked him about the pastimes the Irish had in London. There were at least five Irish halls in the city if I had any interest in dancing, he told me. He wrote their addresses on a piece of paper.

As the evening went on, I was getting used to the work. Out in the evening, I noticed a man in a white coat walking in my direction. I hadn't seen this man before.

'I'm Frank Linski,' he said. 'They call me the Gov. By the way, do you want to work overtime?' he asked me.

I told him I wouldn't be lazy to do an extra bit of work. He told me that there were two extra hours to be done every evening and a half day on Saturday. It was I who was happy to hear this. He left me then and went to talk to somebody else.

I didn't find the week going and, before midday on Saturday, I was well used to the factory and the work that was to be done there. I had no trouble with the work because I could read the blueprints. Some of them that worked there had more trouble avoiding work than they would have had working. There are people like that in every part of the world.

Early on Saturday morning the man with the white coat came back. He stopped for a while talking to George. Then he came over to me.

'Keep up the good work,' he said to me.

I didn't say a word but nodded my head. I could safely say now that I had a permanent job and I'd be inside from the depths of winter. Everybody was waiting for the ringing of the clock at midday on Saturday because that's when we were paid. When the bell was rung everybody was given a brown envelope with their pay in it. I thought that I'd have no pay to get that week because I was only working from the Tuesday. I was given a small envelope, too, and, when I counted the money that was in it, I was fit to jump with joy. Yerra boy, there were thirteen pounds, fourteen shillings and six pence in it. I'd give a month slaving at home for that kind of money.

Some of the workers were complaining that the bonus was small enough that month. I asked George what were they going on about. He told me that there was extra money given out along with the basic pay each month and that that depended on the production of the factory in that month. I asked him how much was in the bonus usually. He looked at the piece of paper that was in with his own pay and he told me that it was twelve pounds this month and that it was a very quiet month. I was thinking that Dónall would be looking for a job in the factory along with me when he heard that. I think he told me one time that he was only earning nine pounds a week after spending six years in college. It's only a fool would go to college breaking his heart and his health if that's the case. Yes, by God, I'd buy myself a new shirt and tie out of my money.

I went into Marks & Spencer on my way home and bought my shirt and tie. I got the fill of my eye of the fine clothes that were on sale there and I noticed that they weren't too dear either. If I bought something every Saturday, it wouldn't take me long to rig myself out from head to foot. Things like that were going through my head as I was walking from Woodgreen to Victoria Road.

I met Dónall on his way down. 'Where are you going?' I asked him, looking at the big scarf that was around his neck. 'Is it because you have a cold that you are wearing that scarf?'

'I'm going to a soccer match,' said Dónall, 'and the colours on the scarf are the colours of Tottenham Hotspur.'

'Wisha, 'twas far from soccer you were reared and what has come over you since you came to this country at all?' I said to him jokingly.

'If you want to come with me to the match, I'll wait for you,' Dónall said.

'I wouldn't cross the road to see them,' I replied.

'You'll get the bug yet, just wait and see,' Dónall assured me.

After dinner I gave myself a good scrubbing. I was determined to get to know London better. I had often heard about Hyde Park. I decided there was no better place to start than there. Instead of taking the underground train, I said I'd use the bus to take me into the centre of the city. When I found out what number bus would take me into the city centre, I went to the place where I would get it and it wasn't long before one came along. It was a double-decker and I went on the upper deck to have a better view. I had to change buses twice to reach my destination and I had to stand the whole way because there was no empty seat.

12

'That's a nice looking shirt,' I said to myself when I looked in the mirror, having put on my new shirt in my room. I was dressing myself for the dance. As I was dressing myself, Dónall came in.

'I thought you had somebody in the room, you were talking so much,' he said to me. I asked him did his team win.

'Yerra, they wouldn't beat the Ballyferriter team today,' he replied. I put a knot on my tie and tied it round my neck.

'What's all this dressing up for?' said Dónall looking at me.

'Faith, I'm going dancing tonight,' I informed him, 'will you come with me?' Dónall shook himself.

'Ah, I won't,' he said. 'Maybe I'll go to the pictures.'

Dónall had no interest in dancing. I had to go on my own without any knowledge of where the dance hall was. Without a doubt, Dónall knew every nook and cranny in the place.

'Manor House is nearby,' he told me. 'Take the tube from Woodgreen and you'll be there inside ten minutes.'

When I was cleaned up, shaved and my hair fixed with Dónall's brylcreem, I stood in front of him.

'Now what would they say to me in Carrachán?' I boasted.

He gazed at me. 'You'll soon know,' he said, 'when you get a letter from home.' I put the key of the house in my pocket.

'I'd better head off,' I said.

When I was crossing the street to Manor House, I could hear the sound of the music from the hall at the end of the street. My heart rose as I came near it. I could hear a fine lively jig. My footsteps quickened with the urge to dance. It put me in mind of the fine summer evenings when I used to cycle down Ard na Carraige. Oh, I was far from Ard na Carraige now. It cost four shillings to get into the dance. The dance floor was black with people and they rising the Lux flakes from the floorboards. I noticed that a crowd of men were sitting up near the stage. I made my way up and sat on a stool. I saw a little way off that there was a room where sandwiches and sweet cakes were on sale.

Just like at home, all the girls were sitting on one side of the hall and the men by themselves on the other side. Any boy and girl who were together, it's up in the tea room they were, sitting at a table. I cast my eye at the fine women who were in the hall and they sitting in one line down the side of it. What was in my head was that I would dance with as many women as I could. 'Twould be the devil if some woman in the hall wasn't living close to Woodgreen. Like the person learning to swim, it is said he shouldn't go in too deep at first. I had the same plan; stay near home until I got used to the place.

I cast my eye on a beauty that I fancied. Yes, the band played an old-time waltz. I got off my stool and made a shape across the hall. There was a good lot of people on the floor already. I asked her to dance and I make out that she only wanted the wind of the word. We wheeled out on the floor. I have to say that she danced as lightly as a bird. A good beginning is half the work. When I asked her where in Ireland she hailed from, she told me she came from the county Laois. She had spent two years in London and she told me that she hadn't noticed me in the hall before. She had no shortage of talk anyway. I told her that I only landed in England the Monday before and that this was my first dance here. Eileen Keane was her name and of course I introduced myself to her. She was surprised when I told her I had a job got already. She was training to be a nurse in Hackney Hospital.

'Where is this Hackney,' I asked her, 'or is it anywhere near Woodgreen?'

''Tis easy to see that you haven't spent much time in London,' she replied. 'Hackney is on the other side altogether.'

That was that and I said goodbye to her after the waltz. Maybe when I got to know the city better, I could get to know her better too. I spent the whole night dancing and it wasn't the same girl I had for any two dances. At the end of the night I was doubtful that any Irish girl was living in Woodgreen or in any place near it. It seemed that they were all living on the other side of the city.

I went into the tea room. I got a cup of tea and a piece of sweet cake and I sat at a table near the counter. Three more sat at the table after a while, a boy and two girls. They were talking and chattering among themselves. The boy was about eighteen years of age and he told me he was from Youghal. My heart rose entirely when he introduced the two girls to me, because one was from Lispole and the other was from Mayo. A quickstep started after a while. I asked the Youghal man which girl was he dancing with, hoping that he was with the Mayo girl because the Kerry girl was a beauty to look at. But leave it to the Cork men when it comes to beauty in women. I was left with the Mayo girl and we went out on the floor.

'Are the Cork fellow and the Kerry girl walking out with each other for long?' I asked the Mayo girl when we were out on the floor.

'This is their first date because he is only two weeks in London,' she replied.

I was fishing away and I didn't want to let on to the Mayo girl that I had a greater interest in the girl from Lispole.

'I suppose you and Máire are in the same flat,' I ventured.

'Not at all,' she replied, 'she's a good bit out because she's working in Hackney.'

'Oh, Holy Mary! She is the second woman I met tonight who's working in Hackney,' I exclaimed. 'I suppose Máire is a nurse too.' She was amazed.

'How did you find out that?' she asked me. 'She'll be finished her course in another year.' I had no luck that night.

'I suppose you're living near her,' I asked the Mayo girl.

'Oh no,' she said, 'I met her on the boat coming over from Ireland this Christmas.'

The dance was ending about this time. We left the dance floor and went over to Tom – that was the Youghal man – and Mary from Lispole. We spent some time talking there.

'The next dance is the last dance,' said my man from the stage.

What would be best for me to do now? Tom made up my mind for me. He caught the Mayo girl by the hand and left Mary and me together. I looked at Mary and she looked at me.

'Well here we go,' I said.

I questioned her closely about who she was and what village in Lispole she was from. After a while I asked her where the Mayo girl was living. Kathleen Joyce was her name.

'Somewhere in Lordship Lane,' she told me.

I was as blind as ever. Mary didn't know rightly where Lordship Lane was and I had even less of a notion as to where it was. When the dance was over we were watching out for the other two.

'Look at them down in the doorway,' Mary said to me after a while. I was getting up my courage by this time.

'Will ye be here again next Saturday?' I asked, pretending to be talking to Tom.

'I'll be here anyway,' said Kathleen. Tom looked at Mary.

'Listen, Mike, are you free next Saturday?' he asked me.

I told him I'd be working until one o'clock in the afternoon.

'Listen,' he asked me, 'did you ever eat dinner in one of the restaurants?'

I told him I didn't.

'Next Saturday evening if the four of us meet, maybe we could sample one of the posh restaurants,' he said.

I wrote down the address of the restaurant where we were to meet.

13

I thought that week was the longest week ever. A long working day and then to come home to my flat with nothing before me but cold walls and half rotten food. Dónall was still talking about looking for a room with cooking facilities, but none of the two of us were putting ourselves out to look for one. We were too tired after our day's work to go out again. Lying on my bed after a long day's work, I thought of the thousands of people who left the coast of Ireland to make their living in foreign countries. People who grew up with the freedom of the glens and the mountains. The song of the birds and the breaking of the waves against the cliffs left behind them. With no sights to see in cities like London but big brick buildings. A black colour on them from the smut of industry. The noise of the machines and the bustle of the people; and yet, loneliness in the middle of the crowd. I was thinking of my father and my mother and they sitting beside the fire, the pipe in my father's mouth and smoke billowing from it.

I was making out that if I spent a year working in London, with the money I was earning I would have the price of my passage to America earned easily and some more besides.

Dónall came in from his own room.

'I was looking through the paper for a room with cooking facilities,' he told me. 'There's a place near Brewers' Grove. Maybe 'twould be no harm to have a look at it.'

I put my two hands behind my head and stretched myself.

'Tomorrow evening maybe,' I replied. Dónall wasn't happy.

'Come on,' he said, 'or we'll be stuck in this hole for the rest of our lives.' I sat up in the bed.

'Where's Brewers' Grove?' I asked him. 'I hope it's not on the other side of the city.'

'It's not,' Dónall informed me. 'It's only a couple of miles from this place. It's near Tottenham Hotspurs' football ground.'

Dónall knew the city well. Why wouldn't he, and he in it a good few years? We took the bus and it only cost us sixpence. When we got off the bus, I looked around. There were six or seven shops in a line.

'There's an awful lot of traffic around here,' I said. 'We won't get a wink of sleep if it's here the room is.'

'Take it easy,' Dónall advised me. 'We have to find Elmhurst Road first.'

We walked about four hundred yards up the street and then turned left.

'Here it is,' said Dónall, 'and isn't it a fine quiet street?'

We found the house and Dónall knocked on the door. A small, thin, washed-out man answered the knock. We asked him had he a room for rent. He opened the door and invited us to follow him. The house had a clean, tidy appearance. The entrance hall was fine and bright and you'd know that somebody was looking after it constantly. We followed him up the stairs and into a room at the top. Yes, it was there in front of our eyes – a fine, spacious, airy room. Nice, bright paper on the walls to lift your heart when you walked in. There were two single beds in it and they had a lovely, comfortable appearance. We asked him how much he was charging for the room and he told us that he charged two pounds, ten shillings per week. Dónall looked at me and spoke in Irish.

'If we were looking forever we wouldn't get a better bargain.

What do you say?'

'Let's take it,' I replied, 'because, God save us, if I have to listen much longer to that strap of a landlady, I'll lose my head.'

We paid a week's rent to the man of the house and told him we'd be back on Saturday.

'Who'll tell the landlady that we're leaving?' I asked Dónall.

'Leave it to me,' he laughed, 'because I have a few more things to say to her as well.'

We walked home and I looked for signs so that I would be able to make my way back here. I had to work a half day the following Saturday and I arranged to meet Dónall in the flat as he had the day off.

On my way home from work that Saturday, I was thinking about my brother Dónall and how he got on. I thought that he would have taken all our belongings to the new room. I hoped to God he had because I didn't want to see the landlady's face that day in particular. I arrived at Elmhurst Road after buying a new pair of shoes on my way home. The room door was open and there was a fine smell of cooking coming down the stairs before me.

'What's on the pan?' I enquired.

'Chops, boy,' came the reply.

'What sort of chops?' I continued. He started laughing.

'These chops are mutton.'

'Are you sure that they're not a piece of an old dog?' I joked.

He told me the story of the morning's adventures.

'Oh, holy Mary!' he began. 'If you heard the landlady when I told her we were leaving! She danced around the house with temper. After all she did for us, she said, and this was her thanks.'

We ate our meal contentedly and 'twas a great consolation not to have her pig's puss across the table from us.

About five o'clock that evening, after scrubbing and dressing myself up, I headed for Kathleen's place in Lordship Lane. We were to meet up with Mary and Tom at seven.

We took the 39 bus from Brewers' Grove into the city centre. We found the restaurant after a little searching. Tom and Mary were waiting for us at the door. In we went and there was a bar there with every kind of drink you could think of. Tom had a pint of beer and the women had some sort of wine. I had a bottle of orange juice. We were informed that we would have to wait for a while. We were talking and chattering to pass the time. At long last, one of the waitresses walked over to us. She told us that our table was ready. Tom was a bit impatient …

'I never had to wait at home like this,' he complained.

We sat at the table. 'Oh, holy Mary!' exclaimed Tom, looking at the table. 'What are all the forks and knives for? We have only two knives and one fork at home.'

'Be quiet,' Mary admonished him, 'anyone would think that this was your first time in a restaurant.' A little smile crossed his face.

'Believe it or not,' he told her, 'but this is my first time ever in a place like this.'

He looked across at her.

'Help me, love,' he pleaded, 'and don't let me make an ass of myself. Which weapon will I start with?'

She handed him the menu.

'Start on the outside and work your way in,' she advised him.

We left it to the girls to order our meal for us. They were more used to this kind of thing. Before long, a bowl of soup was put in front of each of us.

'What kind of soup is this?' enquired Tom, sampling it from his spoon.

'Chicken soup,' Kathleen told him. He looked at her.

'There isn't much chicken in this soup,' he said. 'I make out that the boiling water was left through the chicken.'

The bowls were taken from us when we were finished. Then four big steaming plates were brought to us. There was a small piece of beef on each plate. Tom looked at the plate and then at us.

'I thought I'd have a side of beef on the table in front of me. This wouldn't take the hunger from a cat.'

The waitress came again with four small plates. Two tiny spuds on each plate. No sooner had the plate hit the table in front of Tom than he had his fork stuck to the handle in one of the spuds.

'Bring them in … they are boiled,' he said. The piece of meat that Mary had in her mouth, she blew it out with the dint of laughing. Tom thought that it was for testing them that the two potatoes were on the small plate.

'That's your lot now, boy,' Mary told him, pointing to the two potatoes. 'You're not at home now.'

Then he started to give his litany.

'God be with the days when the pig's head sat with its ears cocked in the middle of the table staring out with those two beady eyes as if it was pleading, 'eat me, eat me!' Then my mother capsizing the big pot next to it and the heap of spuds with the steam rising so high out of them that I could not see my father at the other end of the table.'

There's no doubt but that Tom was a fine talker. A bowl of vegetables was brought in and we started to eat. We ate contentedly and I promise you that Tom wasn't belching when he had finished the meal. When the table was cleared, Tom stood up with his two hands on his head.

'Oh wisha,' he complained, 'this is my first time eating in a restaurant and I can tell you that 'twill be a while before anyone will see me in one again. I'm famished with the hunger still.' We got up from the table when we had paid the bill.

'There's a custom in this country,' Kathleen informed us, 'and that is to leave a tip for the waitress.' Tom wasn't too happy with that kind of talk.

'I will in my eye,' he grumbled, 'and my belly tied to my backbone still with the hunger. Come on, we'll go to the Round Tower.'

This was a dance hall in Holloway Road. It was a bit too early to go dancing when we got to Holloway Road. It was my first time in that part of the city. And so I was depending on the others to guide me.

'Come on,' said Tom, 'we'll go into the Nag's Head.'

The Nag's Head was a pub where all the Irish gathered before they went dancing.

'If you're ever looking for work, this is your place,' said Mary, pushing the door in before her.

Somebody was playing an accordion in a corner of the bar. I was so taken with the music that I let out a fine Gaelic shout that went with the rhythm of the music. Tom pounded the floor with his heel. He ordered a pint of beer for himself.

'Now lads, what are ye having?' he offered. 'It isn't too often I stand.'

The two girls looked at each other. 'Two drops of port,' Mary said after a while.

'And you, Mike?' Tom continued.

'A lemonade,' I told him. 'I never tasted the other stuff.'

'Well, you have to start sometime,' he told me.

I was thinking for a while. 'All right so,' I conceded, 'I'll drink whatever you're having yourself.'

I got butterflies in my stomach when I thought of the pledge I took on the day of my confirmation long ago.

'Did you take the pledge when you were confirmed, Tom?' I asked him.

'The whole school took the pledge,' he laughed. 'The way it was with the priest in our parish, if you didn't take the pledge, he'd read you from the altar the following Sunday. I was nearly sixteen when I was confirmed and I wasn't long out the door of the church when I had a big pint under my head.'

If you saw the look the two girls gave him.

'God forgive you your sins, Thomas McCarthy,' Mary exclaimed. 'There's neither luck nor grace following that kind of mockery.'

He gave two glasses of port to the girls and he shoved a pint of beer towards me.

'Twenty years from now, if I'm a stump of a drunkard falling and rising in some dirty backstreet without clothes or shoes, I'll walk to Youghal barefoot. Then I'll go up on the altar there and declare that it was Thomas McCarthy who was born in that town who made a drunkard out of a poor country boy from Kerry,' I joked.

I took my first sup out of the pint. They were looking at me to see what kind of grimace I would make. But, upon my soul, I didn't let on anything but drank it back like somebody who was drinking for a while.

'Wisha,' I boasted, 'I don't know what all the talk is about this same drink – it tastes like nothing but bog water.'

'Ah, wait a while, Mike, until it begins to work upstairs,' Tom replied, with a fine satisfied appearance on him.

There was a man at the other end of the pub knocking sparks from the floor dancing to the music.

'Didn't you tell me that you could play music, Mike?' Kathleen said to me.

'I can,' I replied, 'but my box is in Ireland and I haven't played a note since I came to London.'

She walked over to the musician and whispered in his ear. He walked over to me with the accordion in his hand.

'They tell me you have a few tunes,' he began. 'Here, sit down and play a reel or a jig. 'Twill give me a chance to drink a pint.'

I took the box and began to play. I wasn't long playing when two pints of beer were put in front of me.

'Who bought those?' I asked Kathleen.

'When a musician is playing in this pub, his drinks are on the house,' she informed me. I was delighted.

'Look at that, boy,' I exclaimed, putting the box down beside me, 'don't they think the world of a musician?' The box player came over to me and took the accordion again.

'Have you any box yourself?' he asked me, putting the straps on himself again.

'Ah no,' I told him, 'I only had a Hohner at home in Ireland. You have a fine box. I suppose it cost a lot of money.'

'They're thirty-five pounds new,' he informed me, 'but listen, I know a man who's selling one at a reasonable price and he didn't play ten tunes on it ever.'

Upon my soul but that put me thinking. I leaned my head in his direction.

'When you say a reasonable price,' I ventured, 'what kind of money would you be talking about?'

He drank a good, long slug out of his pint.

'I'll get it for you for fifteen pounds … On one condition; that you play in the Round House with me every Saturday night.'

My heart jumped. 'Is there any few bob to be made from playing in the Round House?' I asked him.

He put his mouth to my ear. 'Five pounds a man, and keep that to yourself.'

The first thing that ran into my head was that there was a shortage of musicians in the city.

'Is my music good enough for the dance hall?' I asked him.

'Yerra, I wouldn't be asking you if it wasn't,' he reassured me. 'Be here next Saturday night and I'll have the box for you. By the way, are you going to the dance tonight?'

I told him I was. He wanted to find out who I was. I told him. He would be playing for the dance.

'Maybe you'd play a 'Siege of Ennis' for me tonight,' he said. ''Twill get you used to playing there.'

He was Pat O'Malley from the county Mayo. He started to play again. He was a fine, sweet musician. The tunes came very freely to him and every one of them flowed nicely into the next. By the time I had drunk the three pints, I was full to the brim and, as Kathleen said afterwards, I was getting fine and merry and talkative. I stood a drink then.

'Listen,' Kathleen warned me, 'that's your fourth pint and you have no experience of it. Take it easy or your legs will be in the air.'

I took her advice because I was getting afraid that I wouldn't be able to play the 'Siege of Ennis'.

'Come on,' said Mary, nudging Tom who was thinking of making another journey to the well.

We went out. As soon as I got out into the cold air, a kind of light-headedness came over me. My two feet wanted to walk but my brain wasn't in agreement with them. In any case, we got to the door of the hall. When I found myself inside,

I wasn't long making off the toilet. There was nothing in my head but to get to the toilet as fast as I could. I found the bottom of my belly swaying like a sea in a storm shattering against the cliffs. No sooner had I reached the toilet bowl and the door bolted behind me than I threw up the four pints I had drunk. Great God, if this is the life of the drunkard, I wouldn't wish it on my worst enemy. I sat on the toilet seat and a cold sweat came out through me with the weakness. The devil take you, Mike Daneen, it was with manliness that you drew this disaster on yourself. I noticed that there was someone outside the door.

'Are you alive, Mike?' It was Tom McCarthy who had come looking for me.

'Oh wisha, no more than it,' I replied. 'I'll be out straightaway and never again will I be caught like this.'

Tom started to laugh. 'That's what they all say.'

I was coming to myself every second from that on and my stomach was improving. I threw a splash of water on my face and went out towards the dance. Mary and Tom were on the floor before me dancing a waltz.

'Let's dance, Kathleen, my love,' I said to Kathleen.

I noticed that she had a sulky look on her face but, nonetheless, she moved from her seat. We were dancing around and it was I that was doing all the talking. I told her that this wouldn't happen again. That softened things a bit. While we were drinking a drop of tea, the band on the stage took a break and Pat O'Malley started playing. He played the 'Stack of Barley', or the barn dance as that dance was called in England.

'Twon't be long before you'll be going on the buttons,' said Tom. 'The 'Siege of Ennis' always follows this.'

I drank a cup of tea, but, if I got all Ireland, I couldn't look at anything sweet. How could I with the wretched state my stomach was in after the evening?

'Will you be frightened to go on the stage, Mike?' Mary asked me, looking at Pat up on the stage on his own.

'Why would I?' I replied. 'Haven't I given three months of the summer playing on the stage?'

The barn dance finished and everybody left the floor. Pat started to talk.

'There's a musician among us that you haven't heard yet, from Kerry. Here's Mike O'Shea.'

When the crowd heard the word 'Kerry', they gave a big cheer. 'Mike is going to play the 'Siege of Ennis' for ye, so come on up to us Mike.'

I made my way up on to the stage. Pat whispered in my ear.

'They prefer polkas for this dance,' he advised me.

I pulled up the stool to me like any ploughing horse. Pat fitted the straps on my shoulders. There were ten tunes going through my head, but which one would be the most suitable? Then I closed my eyes and thought about Muiríoch Hall. It came to me. Two tunes that Muiris Ó Cuinn used to play when he was playing for a set. This was my first time playing with the help of a microphone. Oh boy, what an ease. I hit every note correctly and got through each tune well. There was shouting and jumping, not to mind Lux flakes rising from the floor. I gave them a fine, long dance and when I finished everybody looked as if they were well pleased, judging by the hand clap I got. Pat came over to me.

'Good man,' he said, 'and don't forget to be at the Nag's Head next Saturday. I'll have the box for you and we'll have a bit of a practice together before we come here.' I went back to my company. My spirits were high again after all that and we went out dancing. We sat down after a while. Tom was telling stories as usual.

'We were so poor at home when I was growing up,' he told us, 'that no shoe went on my legs till I was twelve years old. It took me three months to get used to them. One day they'd be skinning my heels and then when the skin would be toughened a blister would appear on my small toe.' The girls greatly enjoyed that. 'We had no clock at home,' he continued. 'Oh, many's the time I was late for school. But, upon my soul, I always had an excuse.'

Mary spoke then: 'Like the excuses you have for me.'

If I had to tell you all Tom's stories, it would take me a month. Mary was great to get him going. Getting towards the end of the night, a kind of quietness came over him. Mary started picking at him again. Tom had a slightly twisted jaw.

'Was it fighting with someone you were that your jaw is out of joint?' Mary asked him.

Off went Tom composing again. 'I remember well,' he began, 'the day of our confirmation. Whatever fooling I was doing, didn't I let out a big laugh when the bishop stroked me on the jaw. The bishop looked at me suspiciously and said, "I'll take the smile off your face, you blackguard." He gave me another belt and, upon my soul, he put my jaw three inches out of joint with the force of the blow. I can tell you that everyone in the church knew that I was confirmed. I thought I saw the Blessed Virgin going up over my head.'

Kathleen and I took the bus home that night. She didn't open her mouth from the time we left the hall until we got to Lordship Lane. We walked to the gate of the house.

'Will you have tea?' she asked me.

This was my chance. Maybe if I got her sitting on her own, I could find out what was bothering her.

'I never refused tea as you know well,' I answered.

When I found myself sitting at the table with a drop of tea in front of me, I gathered my thoughts together. For fear I'd put my foot in it, I began: 'Kathleen, something is troubling you to-night. Are you still mad at me that I drank four pints of beer?'

'Oh wisha, Mike. Do you think you are the only one who was ever in my company with drink in him? I have been think-ing all morning how to say what I have to say to you. When we were eating dinner I forgot all about it the *craic* was so good.'

Oh boy, what was coming? How is it that when everything is going fine that we're closest to disaster?

'I'd prefer to say this to you so as not to waste your time. I have been thinking for a while about joining the convent.'

I was startled at what I was hearing. 'Why would you want to go into a place like that?' I asked her.

'Ah Mike, I think I have a vocation.'

'I hope I haven't done anything to turn your head,' I said.

'I have to try it,' she continued, 'and I assure you that if I didn't have this higher vocation, it would be hard to separate us.'

What could I say? Everyone is entitled to do what they want. I wished her every luck on the road that was before her. 'I got a letter from a convent in the North of England this week,' she informed me. 'I will be leaving London next week and I'll go to the convent.'

After we had talked for a while, I said I should be going. I promised that I would see her on Tuesday. I left sadly and faced my room.

14

Yes, work was getting more plentiful at United Aircoil and, instead of two hours overtime each week, we were invited to work there every evening and, if we wished, all day Saturday. I was never afraid of hard work, particularly if the pay was good. Why wouldn't I be anxious for work? I was young, athletic and agile with a plan in my head that I couldn't put into effect without money. The loan I got from my old friend when I was leaving home was repaid and a good present with it.

It was the big shop windows that reminded me that Christmas was almost upon us. All the lights and false holly in every window. Santa Claus standing at a street corner here and there, a bucket in front of him, and he looking for money from the people passing by. Children going up to him every one of them with a letter in their hands. I don't know if my brother Dónall got a fit of loneliness, but he made his mind up on the spot that he'd go home for Christmas. The loneliness hit me too but we had only four days off for Christmas. Wouldn't it be nice to be home for the day of the Wren, I was thinking. All of us around the fire on Christmas Eve and the innocence on my brother Tomás' face waiting for Santy. This would be the first Christmas I'd be separated from my family and the house where I was born.

I was talking to Tom McCarthy the week before Christmas. He told me that he wouldn't be going home for Christmas either.

'Listen,' he said to me, 'Mary will be coming to the flat on

Christmas Day. She's going to cook the dinner. Why don't you come to us and spend those few days with us?'

Anything would be better than to be stuck in a room by myself looking at the walls. I told Tom I'd stay with them on one condition; that was that I'd pay my way as regards food and anything else we'd have as well.

'Did you think that you'd get your legs out of it scot-free?' said Tom in high spirits. 'Listen, bring your box with you, we'll have a bit of *craic* on Christmas night.'

On Christmas Eve, the factory was shut at twelve o'clock in the middle of the day. It was just as well because somebody would surely have got caught in one of the machines as most of the workers had a bottle in their lunch-boxes and it wasn't water that was in them.

At eleven o'clock the foremen went around and they told us to take the tools and sweep the floor. Then the boss came out of the office with a big tray full of glasses. Behind him were two men who worked in the office carrying two big cases of beer.

'Drink to the company's health. You have it well earned,' said the boss.

I didn't touch a drop of the whiskey because the memory of the night in the Nag's Head that I drank the four pints of beer was fresh in my mind. I drank a bottle of beer to be mannerly. A lot of the workers went across the road to the nearest pub but I didn't as I had a notion that there was a long night ahead of me. I headed for home and gathered a few clothes together. I jumped into a fine hot tub where I stayed for twenty minutes to take the fatigue of the week from my bones. Yes, Dónall was at home in Carrachán by now and he well stuck into a fine turf fire, I supposed.

My father's two ears would be lit up listening to his description of life in England, but that's life ... I had to be happy with the place I was in.

I was thinking while I was in the tub of the first letter I got from my mother. She was complaining in it about how short my letter had been; it was only like a telegram, that's what she said. But they were well pleased with the five pound note I sent with the letter. If they were mad at me, they never mentioned it in any letter. Oh wisha, 'twould be nice to be at home for Christmas, but that's life. I would have to be satisfied with the place I was in. A priest once said to me in confession that nobody was put into this world to be happy.

I put on a trousers I had bought two weeks before and a white shirt. One of those shirts you can put a clean collar on without changing the shirt itself. They were all the fashion at that time and they were very handy. I put neither kettle nor teapot on the fire, but locked the door and went off with my bag hanging from my shoulder.

Brewers' Grove was black with people rushing at the last minute to buy Christmas presents. I used to think that there were a lot of people in Dingle for the Christmas shopping, but 'twouldn't be a patch on this place. I was looking for a present for Tom. I couldn't go to his place for Christmas with my two hands as long as each other. There were women who were pulling goods from each other. It was plain that they had no shortage of money. I thought of my mother, and other women besides her, buying something in the shop she dealt in all year, hoping for some small present for Christmas.

Tom was shaving himself when I reached his flat. From the appearance of his two eyes, it looked as if he had just got up out of the bed. He gave me a hearty welcome. I threw down my bag at the back of the kitchen and put a case of beer I had brought on the table. He opened a big box that was on the table.

'Look at this, boy,' he said, 'Mary's mother sent her this. And, boy, 'tis hot yet.'

He pulled a fine big lump of a turkey out of the box. Wasn't it a fine sight besides the horse meat you'd swear we were eating for a couple of months. There was the world of noise coming from the bedroom.

'Is Mary in the room, Tom?' I enquired.

'Quiet, quiet,' he said putting his finger to his lips. 'That's the landlady,' he informed me, 'she comes to the flat once a week and cleans the whole place.'

'Look at that now … Is she old?' I asked him.

He told me that she was about thirty-five years old and that she was a widow. It seems that her husband fell down the stairs and was killed on the spot.

'Does Mary know that she cleans the flat once a week?' I asked him.

That puzzled Tom. 'Of course,' he replied. 'Why wouldn't she? Mary will be sleeping with her in the room below tonight.'

The landlady came out of the room. 'That's it now Tom, love,' she said in a strong Cockney accent. She went off down the stairs.

'Yes … Tom love,' I said jokingly. 'Wait till Mary hears that for a story.'

Tom wasn't too happy. 'Things are bad enough, leave it be.'

He then told me that it wasn't Mary who was bothering him. 'Wait till I tell you,' he said. 'I was only a fortnight in this place …' I knew that he had a good story and the two of us sat down beside the table. 'Anyway, the second Saturday I was here I went into the city searching for a barber's shop. I wasn't long travelling when I came across one. I got a fine haircut from the barber and a shampoo too. After I had paid him for his work he stuck two small packets into the top pocket of my jacket. His English was kind of broken. "They are very good – will come in handy for weekend," he said. I thought that they were packets of shampoo and I thanked him and I left it that way. When I came to the flat here, I took them out of my pocket and threw them on the shelf over the fireplace. What I was saying to myself was that they would come in handy when I was washing my hair for the dance.

'A couple of days after that the landlady was cleaning the room and she came across them. I was drinking a drop of tea at the table here when she spoke: "Oh Thomas, you are planning an adventure this weekend!" She had the two packets raised up in her hand. I hadn't a clue what she was on about and I said, "Of course." Oh Mother Mary, but it isn't good to be green. Off she went then, but wait till I tell you. Any time I met her during the week she was almost rubbing herself off me. Saturday came and, as usual, I jumped into the tub for a while and then I went to wash my hair. I took my shampoo as I thought it was. When I had wet my hair, I opened one of the packets. Off I went squeezing it over my head to get out the shampoo. I caught the towel that was hanging behind the door and dried my eyes so that I could examine the shampoo. I put in my two fingers, and what do you think came out?'

Tom studied me to see if I had any understanding of the case. Oh, he had no need to say any more. You couldn't but see those contraceptives in England. He moved back from the table.

'Tis no wonder that the landlady got itchy when she saw them. It would be idle for me to be explaining to her that I was so green I didn't know the difference. I had them up on the shelf and wouldn't any woman think that they were an invitation to come to bed. You know how the English mind operates around things like that.'

I wasn't able to say a word after the fit of laughing I got when I had heard Tom's story.

'What did Mary say when she heard the story?' I asked him.

'Yerra, Mary doesn't know anything about it. What would you do if you were in my shoes?' he replied.

'If she was expecting it, sure maybe I'd knock a turn out of her,' I said to Tom.

'Oh wisha,' groaned Tom, 'no one but a Kerryman would say that.'

I drew up my bag of clothes. 'Here's something small for you for Christmas,' I said. I gave it to him and he gave it the full of his two eyes.

'Ah,' he said, 'a new shirt. 'Twas a stroke of luck that you gave it to me now because I was just going to go out and buy one.'

I threw some steak that I had bought on the table, if you could call it steak. You must understand that the meat was terrible in England in those years. Why wouldn't it be because the best of it was sent to the big houses and 'twas the old cows that were left to the workers.

'Put a strip of it on the pan,' I said, 'my belly is rumbling.'

I hadn't eaten anything from seven o'clock that morning. He put a pot of potatoes on the fire and soon the smell of cooking was all over the house. Then Tom told me that he had invited the landlady to be with us that night.

'She's a good woman and I wouldn't like her to be on her own on Christmas Eve,' he told me. I started to tease him when I heard that.

'Mary will give you the road if you continue to paddle with other women,' I joked. But 'twas hard to knock a start out of him.

'Whatever hour of the night we come home, you go into that sofa over there,' he told me. After we had eaten the steak and potatoes, I threw myself on the sofa to give myself a chance to digest the meal. Tom headed for the tub.

At a quarter to six, the doorbell rang. It startled me. I was dozing and my mind was neither in this world nor in the other world. I opened the door.

'Oh, Mike, are you here already?' It was Mary.

After a while Tom came in and he dressed like a prince. Mary said she'd make a drop of tea for us. 'What would you say to me now?' said Tom, the red tie that he had put on with the new shirt I had given him hanging from his hand. His hair was sleeked back with brylcreem.

'God save us, who gave you the red tie?' said Mary, letting on to be surprised.

'Stop now, Mary girl, that's the colour that's in fashion,' said Tom. 'You'd better run down, Mary, and see if the woman of the house is ready.'

'There's no need to, because I noticed on my way in that she was almost ready,' Mary replied.

I got my accordion and we turned our faces to the stairs. We called on the landlady on the way out. Well, if you saw the clothes she was wearing. Her shoulders and neck were bare, without even a strap to keep her dress up – sure the whole of her breasts were nearly visible. Tom's two eyes were popping out of his head with the dint of staring at her. Mary had to give him a kick in the ankle to bring him to his senses.

'Put your two eyes back in your head,' she warned him. Oh she was a fine woman and the grand smell of perfume from her. Tom introduced us. She looked at me under her eyelashes.

'Hello ducky,' she said.

15

We went to the Elephant & Castle that night. I was playing there some time before in place of a musician from the county Clare who had gone home on holidays. At first we had a drink in a pub near the hall. When I went to stand the first drink, I asked the landlady what was she having. She ordered a drink I had never heard of until then. Pernod and White. We spent an hour and a half drinking and talking. I can tell you that the landlady was knocking them back. The more she was drinking, the more she was shoving into me. I didn't mind, but she was old enough to be my mother. Eventually, Mary got up and said to us that it was time to pay a visit to the dance. Tom was slow to move as always, and you couldn't put a hurry on him. It was a man from Sneem in South Kerry who was running the Elephant & Castle at that time. He used to be a wrestler; one of the famous Caseys. I remember them coming to the Dingle Regatta racing with the Seine boats. No crew would come within an ass's roar of them. They were big, handsome men. Casey was standing at the door of the hall, his backside to the jamb of the door and his arm stretched across to the other frame. His name was Paddy. He had a rough, strong voice and you'd think he was going to eat you with the bark he'd make if anything was annoying him. Narrow legged trousers were all the fashion in those days, particularly with the Teddy Boys. 'Drainpipes' they were called. No one was more of an enemy to Casey than those Teddy Boys. If they came to the Elephant & Castle he wouldn't be long throwing them out again. There were two of them going in ahead of us on this particular night. He caught one of them by the back of the coat.

'Go home and tell your mother to buy you a decent suit and I might let you in next week,' he said to the Teddy Boy, throwing him out in the street. The young fellow didn't even look back because, if he did, Casey would have twisted him in two.

It was Bridie Gallagher, who used to be brought over for Christmas, who was singing that night. She was at the height of her fame then. Everybody was singing her hit song, 'The Boys from the County Armagh'. I had to go on the stage then to play a few tunes as the band were taking a break. When I was going up on stage, the landlady called after me, 'Don't be long, ducky.' Tom was doubled from laughing with every 'ha ha' out of him.

'Bad cess to you and your landlady,' I said in my own mind.

When I had played my few tunes on the stage and had broken a sweat I came back to the table again. Tom was coming back from the counter with a tray full of cups and a big pot of tea.

'Don't let on anything, Mike,' he told me, 'I'm giving an engagement ring to Mary later. I've invited a few people back to the flat after the dance.'

We were walking down the side of the hall.

'What will I do with the landlady?' I asked him, scratching my head.

'Well, do you remember what I said to you earlier in the day?' he said elbowing me in the side. 'Yerra, she's only knocking a bit of a spark out of you.'

We all drank a cup of tea and afterwards we danced a waltz to a fine song from Bridie Gallagher. Whatever Tom said about a bit of *craic*, the landlady, who was dancing with me, was fairly stuck into me going around the floor. Upon my soul but I was in a cold sweat.

For the next dance I went over to Mary and took her out dancing. I left Tom and the landlady together. Upon my soul but this didn't worry Tom too much. The two of them were really circling up and down the hall.

'Do you see those two?' I said to Mary.

'Yerra,' she replied, 'isn't that how all the English are? You think you're still in Ireland. Loosen up and enjoy the night.'

She put me thinking. 'I suppose you're right, Mary,' I conceded.

If there was one person in the flat that night after the dance, there were at least twenty. None of them came dry either. There were cases of beer and cases of porter, bottles of wine and bottles of whiskey and a bottle of Pernod that the landlady brought.

'Take out the box, Mike, and play a few tunes,' someone said to me. I asked about the other tenants and would they be complaining. I was told they were all at the party. I started off with a couple of waltzes and soon a few of them were close dancing in the middle of the room. Mary and Tom came out of the kitchen with a tray full of glasses. She gave me a drink and gave one to the landlady too. She was still following me and now she was sitting beside me. I took one of the glasses of whiskey that was in front of me. 'Twasn't a great beginning. But 'twas as well for me to be feeling the same as them.

When everybody had a glass in their hands, Tom stood in the middle of the floor. He had the appearance of a man who had something important to say. After a while everybody stopped talking.

'Ye all know that Mary and I have been walking out for some time now,' he began. 'Now for her Christmas present I'm going to give her this ring. Mary, come out here.'

Mary came out to the middle of the floor and Tom slipped the ring on her finger.

'I hope you'll accept this from me,' he said, giving her a kiss.

Everybody cheered and there was a lot of kissing for a while. I took up my accordion again and got them out dancing. The drink was given out generously and in a short time everybody was merry. I stayed with porter after drinking the drop of whiskey. I was afraid of whiskey. One man was asked to sing a song. He sang a fine song – 'The Hills of Glen Swilly'. He was a stout man with a white shirt on him and every button on it opened to his belly. His two sleeves were rolled up to his elbows.

'Cor blimey, what a build,' said the landlady, putting her hand on my knee. 'What a build.'

Even though he was well on with the drink, he sang the song well. That was only the start. Because after that everybody had their own song. As there was no other musician in the place but me, I had to stay with the buttons even though I had a mind to dance a set. There's nothing like having the right drink in the right place. Three hours beforehand you couldn't get a word out of anybody but they had music in their feet now, the women as well as the men.

Some of the company were getting a bit bored and I wasn't the only one. I found my music getting slurred and my fingers getting heavy.

'I'm finished playing,' I said to Tom, putting my box away in the corner. He brought me out another bottle.and asked me would I have a drop of the hard stuff.

'Here,' said the landlady when she saw the bottle.

'Holy Mary,' whispered Mary in my ear, 'you couldn't knock her with drink.'

I noticed that it wouldn't be hard to knock a stagger out of Tom. The people started to leave and in the end all that was left was the four of us – me, Tom, Mary and the landlady.

'Come on into the kitchen,' Mary said to her, 'we'll make fine strong tea.' I think she saw the landlady rubbing me with her hand.

'By the devil,' said Tom, 'but you're right for the night.'

I had so much drank that I couldn't care less whether she was there or not.

'Have you any other packet of that shampoo?' I asked him, 'it might come in handy.'

Tom hit me in the back with the palm of his hand.

'Ha ha ha, and you would, too, you bosthoon.'

'Get up or you'll be late for mass!' It was Mary's face I saw when I opened my eyes.

'Where am I? Where am I?' I repeated.

'You're not back in Dingle,' Mary said. 'I was at early mass,' she continued. 'The other drunkard is still stretched. Here now, 'tis as well for you to go to mass… it's Christmas morning.'

The smell of the roast was coming from the kitchen. I got up from the sofa and looked in a mirror that was near me.

'Oh Mike,' I groaned, 'you're dying.'

My two eyes were gone back in my head and my eyelids were swollen.

'Amn't I an ugly looking person in the morning?' I said.

I put my two feet on the ground and looked around for my trousers. After stretching myself a couple of times, I put on my clothes and headed for the bathroom. I got a razor belonging to Tom and it was sufficient to shave me that morning.

'Hurry up! I'm bursting!' Tom was alive and up.

I let him into the bathroom and made for the sofa again but, upon my soul, Mary called out: 'Breakfast is ready.' Breakfast! I'd prefer if it were miles from me because I couldn't look at a breakfast after the night. I sat at the table and, do you know, when I had eaten the first few bites against my will, my appetite came back to me. Tom ate his breakfast as if he had nothing to drink the previous night.

'God bless you boy, you have the courage of a horse this morning,' I said to him, rising from the table. A knock came to the door.

'It's open,' said Mary. It was the landlady. She looked at us and started laughing.

'Listen,' I said to Tom, 'look at her hair. It reminds me of nothing but when the old coat would be falling from our old ass at home.' The landlady didn't hear me at all.

'Have you a spare bottle of milk?' she enquired. Mary took a chair and shoved it in her direction.

'There's fried bacon in the pan and tea in the pot. Sit down.'

Tom looked at me. 'Come on, mass will be starting soon'.

'The turkey will be ready at one o'clock. Don't go on the spree now,' she warned us.

There was a small church about a hundred yards from the flat. I had passed it many times but, God help us, I didn't take much notice of it until now. Looking at it from the outside, you'd think it was an ordinary house. The priest was on the altar when we got in.

'Let us stay near the door,' whispered Tom, 'you'd never know what kind of weakness would come over us.'

It was a small old priest who said the mass and if he didn't have a go at drinking and drunkards during his sermon it isn't day yet.

'This is a spiritual time of the year,' he began. 'It is not a time to be going about the devil's work. When I say the devil's work, drinking comes into that category.'

Tom gave me the elbow. 'He's worse than my mother,' he said.

During holy communion, Tom got up. I thought he was going to receive holy communion.

'Follow me,' he said.

'Where are you going?' I asked him.

'We're going to Lourdes, for the cure.'

'Where is Lourdes or what kind of madness is coming over you?' I asked.

Tom told me again to follow him. We went down a back street and shortly Tom knocked on a small door. Somebody spoke from inside.

'What do you want?' said the voice.

'The cure,' replied Tom. 'Is this Lourdes?'

He must have said the right thing because the door opened. The barman knew Tom. He asked him who was with him and Tom introduced me. We walked in to a long dark hall and then through a door. We were in some pub and from the look around I gave, it was all Irish who were in there. None of them were too healthy looking that morning any more than ourselves.

'Listen, Tom,' I said, 'you know that Mary will have the dinner on the table at one o'clock.' Tom looked at his watch.

'We have an hour and a quarter, we'll be well cured by then,' he replied.

Most of the people who were there I recognised from the dances, but I hadn't names for half of them. The first salute I got from a big block of a man who had his tie loosened well out from his neck was, 'Where is the box?'. Tom got a couple of small ones and he handed one to me.

'Here,' he said, 'this will straighten your jaw and don't mind my jaw because nothing could straighten it.'

There were four men at the bottom of the bar playing darts.

'Holy Mary,' said Tom, rubbing his eyes, 'how do they see the numbers at all?'

We sat at the counter at our leisure, beside four men from the county Mayo. We were talking about work. That was the first morning I found out where I'd face if I was looking for work on the buildings.

'Look around you,' said Tom, 'half of these won't eat a Christmas dinner today. Their dinner is in front of them.'

I shook my head in surprise. 'Twas hard for me to believe that anybody would go so low that he'd abandon food with the craze for drink.

'Oh wisha,' I said, 'I wouldn't like to be depending on them tomorrow to dig a trench. My father always said that a good horse must be well fed.'

Tom jumped off the stool. 'Come on, boy,' he exclaimed, 'or the leg of the turkey will be burned. I didn't eat a pick of a turkey since last Christmas.'

We said goodbye to the company and went out the back door again.

16

'When the goat gets into the temple, he doesn't stop till he goes on the altar.' That's how the old saying goes and believe every word of it from me. I gave January and February working for United Aircoil. I was working ten hours a day and Saturdays as well. They had so much work that they were thinking about having work on Sunday also, but they put it out of their heads because if some of the workers got all England they wouldn't give up their free Sundays. There was no week but twenty pounds clear went into my pocket and a bonus at the end of the month as well. But isn't it strange – no matter how much a person has, the grass is greener on the other side of the ditch. I suppose that's the devil working in us from time to time. Going on for the end of March, the cold and frost of winter were gone and the days were stretching. You'd hear nothing at the dances and in the pubs but talk about digging and putting down foundations. More people building castles in the air. Yes, by God, building and big money. I can tell you that cement was mixed at the counter of the Nag's Head and it was poured deeply underground. As Pat O'Malley, who was in my company one Saturday night, said to me: 'Do you hear that talk all around you, Mike? That's a fever that comes on us at the end of spring, when the days are getting longer and the weather is softening'.

That same evening I got the 'start', even though I wasn't looking for work on the buildings. There was a middle-aged man going from person to person asking them to work. He had the nose of a drunkard and his face looked like someone had opened a trench or two in it at one time in his life.

'Look at that,' said Pat whispering in my ear. 'How things have changed. A couple of years ago you'd have to be pumping drink into that man to get an answer out of him. 'Twill make a great year for the buildings.'

Your man came over to us after a while. By the way Pat and he saluted each other I'd say they weren't too thankful to each other.

'Are you still picking the heels off of the rookies, Liam, or are you getting too old?' said O'Malley.

Your man snarled and he started to talk to me.

'My name is Liam Kavanagh. I'm working for Murphy's. There's a big construction site starting down in Camden Town. There'll be work there for a year. If that place is too far from where you live we have six other sites around the city.'

I let him talk away and when he had finished I asked him: 'How much a week do Murphy's pay?'

He gave a while thinking.

'That's up to yourself. It's all piece work. 'Twould be a bad week you wouldn't bring home thirty pounds. I'm talking now about navvies.'

When I heard thirty pounds a week, that's all I needed.

'I have to give a week's notice to the place where I'm working,' I said.

He put his hand on my back. 'I like a man with principles,' he replied. He gave me a card with the address of the place in Camden Town and he wrote his name on the top of the card.

'Contact the man in the office and tell him I sent you,' he told me.

He took my name and address and went off to somebody

else. Pat stuck his head in my direction when your man had left.

'Mr O'Shea,' he said, 'you'll regret the day you took a job from that tinker.'

He didn't say any more and there was no point in quizzing him. The way my head was working and I putting things together 'twould be the devil altogether if the work in Camden Town didn't last till the end of summer. With the big pay, I'd have put aside the fare to America and a little bit with it.

After leaving United Aircoil the following Friday evening, I bought a fine strong pair of steel-tipped boots and overalls. The working clothes I had were well worn and there was a crust on them from the oil that was on the copper pipes. What I was thinking on my way home on the train was that it was a long time since I had handled a shovel. I'd have blisters for the first week.

Early on the Monday morning after that I had to turn my face to the bus. Because of that, I had to leave my flat half an hour earlier than usual as the buses were a lot slower than the train. I had no bother making off the site because half the men who got off the bus in Camden Town were heading for the same place. I enquired from one man where the office was and he put me in the right direction.

'Over there,' he said showing me a small cabin. 'And watch out for Sweeney, he has a fine head on him after the weekend.'

I knocked on the door.

'Come in. Do you think this is a hotel? Push it in in front of you,' was all I heard.

'Holy Mary,' I was thinking, 'what kind of a pig is this at all?'

I took the card out of my pocket and gave it to him. He looked at the card and he looked at me.

'Have you a trade?' he asked me.

'I have,' I replied, 'I'm a navvy.'

'You have an educated tongue as well,' he said. 'Find Colm Naughton. He's working on one of the cement mixers. Here's the tool of your trade.'

He handed me a shovel that had a small, short handle on it.

'Clean that every evening before you go home,' he told me, 'and don't lose it or you'll have to pay for a new one out of your own pocket.'

I went out the door without saying another word. A black man who was working outside steered me over to the other side of the site.

'There are sixteen mixers working over there,' he said. 'Colm Naughton has to be in charge of some one of them.'

I put my shovel on my shoulder exactly as if I were earthing the spuds at home and walked across the site. When I asked two men who were shovelling into one of the mixers where was Colm Naughton they showed me a mixer with only one man in charge of it. When I reached the mixer, I took the shovel from my shoulder.

'Are you Colm Naughton?' I asked him.

'Are you the new navvy?' he answered me. 'Well, if you are fall in on the other side of me here. Now, it's four shovels of gravel and then one shovel of cement.'

I started working my shovel.

'You're left-handed,' he observed. 'We'll go well together because I work right-handed.'

I introduced myself. He told me to keep working at the same speed as himself because it was a long day until evening.

A man would come with a barrow and it would be filled from the mixer. He'd go in a hurry up the plank until he disappeared from view up on the second level.

'That's hard work,' Colm said to me, pointing to the man with the barrow. 'There was an Englishman working with me for a fortnight. He thought that the work was too hard and no one has seen him since the middle of the week. Only for that, you'd be pushing that barrow.'

Nobody came near us for a while. Soon I saw the man who spoke to me in the Nag's Head a week before making for me. He was shouting at four men who were putting up wooden forms.

'Look at that fellow,' said Colm. 'He's the biggest bastard of a blackguard that was ever in charge of workers. I never heard him praising a man only always condemning.'

I didn't have to wait long to find out the truth of that story. He ordered Naughton to shovel faster and not to have 'the young man as lazy as yourself'. But Naughton advised me not to pretend that I heard him at all because he wouldn't come within ten feet of him.

'If he did,' he said, 'he'd get the edge of the shovel down on his head.'

I didn't say a word but kept my head down and worked away. Your man spent ten minutes there with his two arms folded looking at us. Empty barrows were coming and full ones going away. Then he took the barrow from one man and put it under the mixer again. Naughton didn't spare the cement because he filled the barrow to the top. The man went off at speed up the plank. There was a man up there before him he thought was too slow. He let a fearsome shout out of him: 'Can you work any faster, you lazy bastard? Your mother should have drowned you when you were a baby.'

'Look at that poor unfortunate,' said Colm, 'and the abuse he got from that blackguard. This is his first day on the job. Oh wisha, that fellow will come to a bad end and I hope to God I'll be around to see it.'

I was thinking how lucky I was to have this fine man here beside me as my partner. At half past ten on the dot, the mixers were stopped. We had twenty minutes for tea. Colm washed his shovel and I did too.

'Come on, there's a canteen over there. Did you bring any food with you?' he said.

I took my coat. 'I have a couple of sandwiches in my pocket,' I replied.

My partner advised me: 'Take your shovel with you or you'll be without it. Your eye would be picked out of your head if your back was turned.'

There was a gas ring in a corner of the canteen. Colm had it soon lit and had the back of the shovel laid on it. He took a pound of sausages out of a small bag and spread them on the top of the shovel.

'Who'd bother to buy a frying pan?' he said with a smile on his face.

'Yes wisha, Mike will see more,' I said to myself. 'Twas no wonder he gave the shovel a good cleaning before he came in.

'Now,' said Colm, 'get half a dozen of those and be chewing away.' He turned the shovel upside down on a small table.

''Twas to Mike I spoke,' he said, and, when I turned around, I saw that he had caught the hand of a man who was reaching for the sausages. When we had filled our bellies with sausages and strong tea we went out again and there was little hunger on us from that to lunchtime.

Liam, the straw boss, came by several times during the day and it wasn't to praise us he came. 'Fill your shovel' or some nonsense like that was what he came out with. Many times during that day Pat O'Malley's advice came back to me when he told me I'd regret coming to this place.

Because I wasn't used to working with a shovel for some time, every bone in my body was sore that first night. My two hands were full of blisters as well. But, like anything else, I was toughening up every day I gave working there and soon the skin on my hands got hard and my bones got used to the work. I was a fortnight working there before I got my first pay. I couldn't wait to see what was inside in the little red envelope. I wasn't very pleased when I counted out the money. I had only about two pounds more than I was making in United Aircoil. I was thinking what an eejit I was to have left it at all. Me standing beside a mixer from morning till night shovelling gravel and cement into it and if there was any puff of wind at all there would be no recognising me in the evening because the cement would be stuck on to my clothes and my skin. I had to hop into a tub of hot water every evening when I'd come home in order to wash myself properly. My two hands were split and burned from that same cement.

I spent the whole summer working with Colm. Men would come and, if they did, many of them would be in a hurry to leave again. I never again saw a job that so many workers left. That was no great sign of the men who were in charge.

June came very hot that year. I remember it well because there were about forty bricklayers building and not enough labourers to draw the bricks to them. Not all the cement mixers were needed, it seems, because this particular morning the straw boss came to us. He gave us orders not to mix any more cement in the mixer and when the last barrow was filled from it to clean it out well because it wouldn't be needed for a while. We would have to go drawing bricks to the brickies. They had gone to the third floor with their work.

'The height might pardon you two lazy bastards,' he swore at us.

Colm was going to hit him only I caught his hand. Your man went away without another word.

'Oh wisha, before this job is finished I'll break his head against some wall,' said Colm angrily.

We washed the mixer and our shovels and returned them to the man in the hut. We got a hod apiece. Colm advised me to bring a bit of a blanket the following day so that the hod wouldn't take the skin off my shoulders with the weight of the bricks.

The following morning, I watched the way Colm put the bricks on the hod. He put them across each other so that they wouldn't fall off when he was climbing. He told me to follow him up the first few times and to watch how he laid the bricks. The brickies would get annoyed if everything wasn't just so for them. If you heard me complaining before about the cement getting stuck on me, I admit that things were hard at times but I got used to it. But, upon my soul, before evening fell on my first day carrying the hod, I understood well the talk the people who were at home on holidays had about the hard work it was carrying the hod. The calves of my legs were fit to burst, my two hands were tired and sore and my shoulder was stinging because it was skinned from the weight of the hod. No doubt it was because I wasn't used to it. I was no more than able to put one foot in front of the other that evening when I was walking from the bus because the two cheeks of my arse were full of windgall after the sweat of the day and they were irritated as a result. Colm came to my rescue once again. He told me to rub the stuff you put on your face after shaving to my backside and I'd be fine in the morning. That man never put me astray.

I went into the barber's shop on my way home and bought a bottle of that stuff from him. One thing Colm didn't tell me, however. That's the pain and crucifixion that would come upon me after I applied the stuff at first. I was inside in the toilet putting the stuff on me when I shouted out with pain.

'What in the devil is wrong with you or are you hard in the belly?' asked my brother Dónall, coming to the door of the toilet.

At this time I was shouting and jumping around the small room like somebody being burned in a fire. After a while I got some little relief. Dónall was still outside asking me what was wrong with me.

'Is it the way that you have cut your throat with the razor?' he was saying now.

Ah, the relief. Yes, boy, your man was right when all is said and done. Upon my soul it was better than any ointment that would come out of a doctor's bag. When my backside was all right again, I got a bit of an old blanket and spent the night sewing it together to make a small pillow that I could put between the hod and my shoulder.

Like every other kind of work, I got used to the hod and I didn't mind it after a while. But I was sorry for Colm because he wasn't as young or as active as me and he found the work fairly hard. In this kind of work, however, there was no pity for the weak man or the man whose health wasn't too good. They were trying to knock as much work as possible out of everybody and if you weren't able to do the work there was nothing for you but the sack.

To make things even worse, the weather got very hot in June that year and the heat-wave lasted till the end of August. We were so roasted from the sun that our skin was red-black. I often took notice of our straw boss. Even though he never did any work but swear and shout at us, the sweat came out through him like juice would come out of a pig you'd be roasting over the fire.

'Look at that ass,' Colm used to say, 'that's beer coming out through him.'

The work wasn't going as fast as the company would have liked. The heat that summer was unusual and because of the heat wave the workers weren't able to keep working at their normal speed. The straw boss spoke to Naughton one morning.

'Naughton,' he said, 'if you can't keep up with the rest, get a job working with a crowd of women.'

The boss was in the horrors from drink that same morning. Naughton did nothing but let a grunt out of him. He was behind me the rest of the morning talking to himself. It was easy to see that he had come to the end of his patience and it was no wonder because he was heart-scalded from that blackguard of a boss. I was trying to pacify him but it was no use. I saw him unloading his hod with daggers in his eyes.

Just before lunch we were going up to the second level when we heard a shout from the top of the scaffolding.

'Watch out for the brick,' somebody shouted.

Everybody looked to see where the brick was falling. I heard a groan coming from somebody near me and when I looked around, there was a man in a heap on the ground. Everybody was enquiring who he was.

'Call the doctor and the ambulance – his head is split,' somebody shouted.

It took a few minutes before we found out who was on the ground.

'It's the straw boss that's hurt,' said one of the brickies.

I looked at Colm who was near me to see how that went down with him. I'd swear I saw a smile on his face. If there was, he said nothing to anybody. It wasn't long before a doctor and an ambulance came and we got the order to go back to work. I asked Colm if he saw the brick falling. His talk had come back to him again.

'Listen,' he said, 'there's power in God's hand yet.'

He put his hod on his shoulder and off he went down before us and you'd swear he was a young boy again.

No tears were shed for the fellow who was taken to the hospital. 'Twas true for the man who said that the heart hardens against the world that hardens it. I saw no trace of the straw boss from that day to this. I heard from somebody that he came to himself but he never again did a day's work.

17

The room opposite us in our flat was vacant and the man of the house was looking for tenants for it. That same man never interfered with us and you'd see from his appearance that the health wasn't too good with him. One of the neighbours said to me when we were talking across the fence that he gave years in prison during the war in a German prisoner of war camp. I well believed that because any time I spoke with him, I noticed that he was on edge. Within a week he had got tenants for the room. He was very pleased with himself. 'Nice Irish boys' he told me it was that were coming. Yes wisha! 'Nice Irish boys'. One of them was a lump of a blackguard from Clare and his mate was a blackguard from Sligo. They had no shortage of money because they were working on a cable line somewhere in the north of the city.

There was no evening they came in that they hadn't a good drop taken. They were always short of something in their own flat and they were always bumming off of us. They were the most worthless and badly mannered pair I came across since I started to understand what bad manners were. You never heard such a commotion as used to come from that room every night and early in the morning, particularly at the weekends. A quick end came to the peace and quiet we had since we came to our room first. I couldn't understand how the man of the house hadn't spoken to them about it. Many's the time they left me with little sleep.

One night when I was coming home from the dance, I heard

an awful commotion as I got near our flat. I knew well that the racket was coming from their room. 'Twas the very devil if the man of the house didn't hear the racket tonight. When I was going past their room, I noticed that the door was half open and I gave a quick look inside. There were only four in the room; the two men and two women of the street that they picked up some place or other. There was a bottle of some kind in the middle of the table and the two women were sitting on the men's knees. I never heard such noise from any four before.

'We'll have to speak to the man of the house,' Dónall said to me when I reached our room.

I set the alarm clock for eight o'clock the following morning. I was getting a haircut and then I was going to the tailor to try on a suit he was making for me. We went to bed but, God help us! twould have been as well for us to be idle. Dónall was going to go out and them to tell them to be quiet, but I stopped him. From what I saw of their kind in the pubs, they wouldn't be long in giving you a black eye. All they wanted was fighting and arguing. I had to get up out of bed in the end and turn on the light. I picked up a newspaper. But 'twas worse the prancing in the other room was getting. If Dainín Dan, my father, got hold of their likes, he wouldn't be long straightening their faces or breaking their backbones. I gave a long time reading the paper and, when I looked at the clock, I could see it was making for five in the morning. Oh wisha! The two out-and-out blackguards. More time went by and there was no letting up from them. Then I heard footsteps heading for their room. I opened the door a fraction to have a look at the other room. It was the man of the house that was there and he in his night shirt. I couldn't make out what he was saying to them but it was all the same for him because the two blackguards were only laughing at him. One of them was threatening him with a knife or some such weapon and then he threw it. Then the ructions started. The poor man was telling them to leave the house at once. All he got for an answer was, 'Fuck off down where you belong, you effin' Polack.' With that the two caught hold of him. They lifted him clean off the ground and ran him to the top of the stairs. One of them gave him a kick in the backside and shoved him down the stairs. He went head over heels from the top to the bottom and even though he tried to catch hold of the banisters, his grip slipped.

'O, Holy Mary,' I said, closing the door silently. Dónall asked me what happened and I told him.

'Right wisha,' I said making for my bed, 'we'll lock the door now because I'd say we'll see peelers by morning.'

The clock woke me at eight. After I had eaten a light breakfast, I said to Dónall that I was going out to get a haircut. When I got to the barber's he was hard at work with three men waiting for haircuts. After a while the barber called me over to him. I told him to wash my hair as it was full of cement after the week. He started to work on me and it wasn't long before he was finished. When my hair was washed and dried he pulled out a bottle. What was in the bottle was stuff to kill head lice and I can tell you that there was a fair stinging from it. I'm not saying now that they were on my head but that stuff was used at the time just in case. I could see out on to the street and the people walking outside. Coming down the side of the street on the other side I saw a small figure of a man running like he was trying to get away from somebody. As he was coming nearer to me I imagined that I should know him. The barber brushed the back of my head with a small hand brush. He charged me four shillings for his work.

By this time the man I was watching was directly across from the barber's window. '

As sure as I'm alive, it's Dónall that's there,' I said to myself.

He ran across the street and looked in through the window. He was panting and his face was as white as if he had seen someone from the other world. I went out the door.

'We-We-' Dónall couldn't say any more with the panting.

I asked him what was up.

'We're after being evicted from the room,' he said when he got his breath back. I asked him why so. He answered that the peelers had come that morning and the two in the other room were arrested. Although he was badly shaken, the man of the house wasn't too badly injured after all the abuse he got.

'One of the peelers knocked on the door,' Dónall told me, 'and he said that the man who owned the house gave orders that the house was to be cleared by evening.'

I asked Dónall had he told the peelers that we had nothing to do with the blackguarding and he told me that he did but the peeler said that the man of the house had given firm orders not to let any Irish into the house ever again.

'What'll we do now? It'll take us at least a week to find a decent place. Have we much time left to clear our of the room?' I asked.

'Two hours,' Dónall replied. 'The peeler said we didn't have to go for a week but from the appearance of the man of the house 'twould be as well for us to get out fast.'

Dónall put his hand on my shoulder. 'Come on,' he said, ''tis as well for us to throw the old clothes together and clear out of the place in the name of God.'

We walked up to the flat without a word out of either of us. There was no trace of the man of the house when we were making our way up the stairs. When we had everything ready, I looked around the room.

'Yes, where will we turn our faces now?' I said, scratching my head. Suddenly it dawned on me.

'Come on, I have it,' I exclaimed. We left the two keys at the bottom of the stairs near the owner's door.

When we were walking down the street, Dónall spoke: 'You didn't tell me what solution you have for our problem,' he said.

I put my case and accordion down on the pavement.

'Now,' I said, 'where do I go every Saturday? To the barber isn't it? He has a small room at the back of the shop. We'll leave the cases there and we'll be able to go looking for a room then without being loaded down.'

When we had left the cases in the room, Dónall said that it would be better for us to have a bite to eat first and then to search through the paper. When we had eaten, I handed the newspaper to Dónall. I told him that he was the scholar and to cast his eye over the ads and if he saw any suitable address to call it out and I would write it down. He spread the paper on the table and he ran his finger down through it. He gave me about five addresses in all.

'The room nearest us is up in Lordship Lane near Wood-green. We'll start there,' he said. We took to the road.

We looked at a dozen rooms that day. A while walking, a while on the bus, a while on the tube. One room was too damp, another too congested, another room too big. All the trouble we took but there was no cure for it. I couldn't put those two blackguards out of my head. It was just like the sins of our fathers coming down on us. It follows everybody from Adam and Eve down. Dónall looked at his watch.

'It's half past four and we have no place got yet. What will we do?' he asked.

I spoke: 'Look at that pub across the street. We'll go in there and we'll drink a pint. My throat is dry and my feet are on fire.'

That startled him.

'When did you start drinking, you devil?' he wanted to know.

I said that 'twas all the one to him but to follow me. He took my advice. After taking a good slug out of his pint, Dónall said: 'Now where will the deer go?'

I asked Dónall had he any money put aside. He grinned and told me that was a very personal question. I told him that I wasn't being nosey but was trying to make out if the had the price of the passage to America. He told me that he had and a bit besides.

'I have the price of my passage over too,' I informed him. 'Now we've nothing better to do than to get a reasonable hotel for a week until we put everything in order. Next Saturday we'll hit for home and we'll get ready to go to America.'

Although Dónall seldom agreed fully with me, he did this time. He stood up.

'Come on,' he exclaimed, 'and we'll get our bags from the barber before he closes.'

We got a room in a small hotel near Woodgreen that evening. One pound five shillings a night and only the breakfast was included. We were barely in the hotel when Dónall took out his pen. We didn't want to give them too much of a surprise at home. They got a big enough fright when I hit for England the first time. I went to the Round Tower where I was playing that night. I would have to say goodbye to all my friends. Without a doubt, but for what happened that morning I would have stayed in London a while longer. But the worst thing that can happen may turn out to be the best thing in the long run. Maybe if I spent another six months in London I'd get too fond of it and I'd stay there altogether.

On Friday morning we left Paddington Station and turned our faces across the country towards our home village.

18

When the train pulled into Tralee station on Saturday morning, the Dingle bus was waiting for it. Yes, the worst part of the journey was over us and we were tired out. The sea was very rough when we were crossing the night before. Along with that, we had two long train journeys on both sides of the sea. Our bones would get relief when we would lie back on a fine feather bed at home.

The bus pulled out of the station and down towards the town. Even though Tralee is a busy town, it's only a little village compared to London. We went out from Tralee on the Dingle road. There was very little traffic to be seen going into or out of the town. The rails of the Dingle railway were on our left and nettles growing out of them. Why wouldn't they, for no train ran on that line since 1953. It was the Basin, a little man-made cove, that was used years before this to bring goods in from Tralee Bay to the shopkeepers and other companies. There wasn't even a seagull swimming on it now.

Blennerville Bridge narrowed and crooked before us, the bus going from Blennerville over the west Kerry mountains. I always liked to cast my eye on the highest peak rising from the sea and to think that it was in the parish at the other side of it that I was born. Of course, it's Mount Brandon I'm talking about.

'You're very quiet,' Dónall said to me as the bus was heading for Camp village.

'I'm taking in sights now that I never noticed before this no matter how many times I passed them,' I told him.

Before us was the first bad bend at Camp Bridge. Above us, the high railway bridge. I used to hear my father talking about one time before I was born the train went off that same bridge. It was said that there were pigs in one of the carriages and the people of the place were in luck. It was said afterwards that some of the Camp farmers had sows and bonhams in plenty. Maybe the two stories had nothing to do with each other.

Going down Gleann na nGealt, the sight would lift your heart. Below you is the most beautiful valley in Ireland. Down in that valley is the well, Tobar na nGealt, that I heard the old people talking about. Up through Luachair and down near Sliabh Mór were the bogs that put smoke in every chimney from Blennerville to Lispole. Their turf was as good as any coal that ever came out of Newcastle. My hand was on my chin and my thoughts were running with the fall. Down into Annascaul. I had often heard about the river that flows under Annascaul Bridge. Many's the salmon poor misfortunes pulled out of it who hadn't any other way of making a shilling.

Then into the most scenic part of the road; made scenic by the world and by the weather. Hills and hollows, the small horseshoe bend and the big horseshoe bend. Farmers going the road with their horses and carts and rails full to the brim with turnips. The farmer behind the horse raising his hand to salute everyone who passed by. There wasn't a cloud in the sky when we reached the top of Garraí na dTor. It was there that I fully realised I was nearing home. Baile an Ghóilín tower visible and the Coill Mhór at its foot. That's where Lord Ventry used to live. The building that I'd wonder at when I'd come from Dingle a few years before this because of all its windows. That's Lord Ventry's house, or Coláiste Íde today.

The straight road in from Lispole … A road of hollows and

potholes. The race field at the turn of Baile an tSagairt – it was said that there are twenty-nine acres in that field. There was great talk among the old people about a man who mowed that field with a scythe in twenty-eight days. Upon my soul but he had energy.

'You're looking out the window since you left Tralee. You'd swear it was the first time you ever travelled this road,' said Dónall to me, taking his jacket down from the rack in the bus.

'But, boy, it's the first time I have travelled this road with my two eyes open,' I replied.

The bus drove up the main street in Dingle and stopped outside Atkins' shop. That was its final stop of the day.

'Look at her outside,' said Dónall, pointing out through the window.

When I looked out I saw that it was my mother he was talking about. She was there waiting for the door of the bus to open. I let Dónall out before me because it ran through my head that she would turn on me for going to England without saying a word to her or to my father. She put her two hands around him and the tears fell from her eyes.

'Welcome home,' she cried. She looked at me. 'Oh you devil, I should box your ears. Why didn't you tell us you were going to England after the match?' I answered her.

'If I did,' I said, 'I'd be in Carrachán yet with my finger in my mouth.' We took our cases out of the back of the bus.

'I suppose we had better get a hackney car,' Dónall offered.

My mother said that she had one engaged already and she walked down towards Jack Dillon's butcher's shop.

'Listen, Dónall, leave everything to her or you'll have no peace,' I advised him.

We went into Jack Dillon's butcher's shop and we bought

fresh meat, bacon and sausages to have when we got home.

My mother never stopped asking us questions from the time we left Dingle until we stopped at the gate of our house. I asked her where was the old fellow when we were walking in the pavement. I thought it strange that he wasn't at the door.

'He was working over in Baile an Ghainnín Beag,' she told me, 'but he should be at home by now.'

I put my head in over the threshold. The smoke from his pipe was rising in clouds from the corner as was usual.

'That tobacco will kill you,' I said walking into the middle of the kitchen. He took the pipe out of his mouth and looked at the two of us with his shrewd eyes.

'The stormy kettle coming for shelter.' That's the salute we got. 'Upon my soul but ye have a sheen on ye from the horse meat,' he continued. 'It was always said that it was more wholesome than beef.'

I put my case on the table and opened it. I took out the pipe I had put on top of my clothes and gave it to him.

'Here's a fine pipe,' I said, 'and may the bit of a stem on that pipe you have yourself not burn the face off of you.'

My mother put the frying pan on the fire and it wasn't long before we had a fine feed of bacon and sausages in front of us. We hadn't eaten long when Tomás, my young brother, came up to Dónall.

'Is there anything in those cases for me?' he asked. Dónall started to laugh.

'Wait till Mammy clears the table. Maybe we'd get something small for you,' he said.

My father took the bag of little sods that was against the wall and built up the fire. There were stories to be told and questions to be asked. It reminded me of the time when we were all children. A big fire would be put down always when Grae came in to tell his stories. My mother cleared the table and swept the kitchen. Tomás was sitting impatiently.

'Will you open your case now?' he asked me in a whisper.

'Give it here to me,' I told him.

He wasn't long going for it. I started to search for the box that had a pair of football boots in it. When he took the cover off of it after I gave it to him, I thought the two eyes would jump out of his head.

'Up Cuas! Football boots, by God,' he said. His two feet nearly got tangled when he was taking off his old boots.

'Oh wisha,' my father said filling his pipe, 'the window pane will be tried and tested now.'

That was nothing until Dónall gave him what he had bought for him himself.

We spent the evening sitting by the fire and if we weren't quizzed about everything that happened to us since we left it isn't day yet. Without a doubt all we told them was that everything was better than the next in London. Some little things they were better off not hearing and we kept those to ourselves. My father had little to say only taking in everything. After a while he sat back in his chair and he spoke.

'I gave half a year in England myself,' he began, 'and I understood that half the people there had neither religion nor conscience. Even the Irish. There was a lot of them that never went near a church from one end of the year to the other.'

My mother looked at him and then she looked at us.

'Well, is the country that bad?' she enquired.

Dónall answered. 'Well, that's up to each person; there's a church on every corner and confession every night.'

Dainín let a long cloud of smoke out of his mouth.

'There is, and the devil at the other corner trying to tempt you.' I changed the subject.

'Have you the last of the potatoes dug yet?' I asked him.

He told me they were dug with a week. Then Dónall started questioning him about the neighbours. I had to laugh when he asked him how was Meex. This was the neighbour who had a twisted little finger from trying the hens, or at least that was what was said. The thing that was funny about it was Dónall asking about him and we having an account of his death in a letter we got from home a couple of months before this. My father spoke then: 'If you meet him, don't stay with him,' he joked. My mother had to put her apron over her face with the laughing.

'Oh, Dónall, I sent the forms to Dublin and an answer came back yesterday. You'll have to be examined by a doctor a week from Tuesday,' my mother said. Then she asked me had I the price of my passage put aside yet. I told her I had. My father and mother looked at me in surprise.

'Mike is no fool,' they exclaimed.

I got up out of the chair to stretch my bones. 'I'll fill out a form tomorrow,' I said, anxious for the road. 'I have no business here scratching my backside.'

My mother folded her arms. 'You needn't,' she informed me. 'You're under eighteen and you can go over on your father's passport.'

My father was an American citizen because he had spent ten years over there. All I had to do was to go to Cork and they'd make all arrangements.

'Ye're better off in America,' my father said, 'because ye'll all be together. I never liked England and I wouldn't advise any young lad to spend time there.' We were talking and gossiping until well into the night. In the end I found my two eyes closing with fatigue and with sleep.

'I'm going under the blanket,' I said, bidding them good night and heading for the bed.

I gave the next week wandering around the place. I had visited all the neighbours and I was getting impatient again. When a person is used to be working every day, he wouldn't have much patience being idle. I was every day watching for the postman, waiting for a call to Cork. It came the second week I was at home. My father had to go with me because it was on his passport I was going to America. Wasn't I the lucky one that he took out citizenship when he was over there. We didn't have a half an hour's delay in that small office in Cork. I didn't have to undergo doctors or questioning. All I had to do was sign my name at the bottom of the passport and I was an American citizen as well, even though I had never put a foot in that country. Dónall got on well too, but he had to go to Dublin about the papers. However, his papers were ready inside three weeks. Then the two of us faced into Tommy Galvin's office in Dingle to buy our tickets.

Our flight was arranged for 20 October 1959. A Pan Am plane was leaving Shannon Airport on that day. When I was packing my case, many things ran through my head. A week's pay wouldn't bring me home from the place I was going to. You could see the loneliness on my mother's face when we were getting ready for the road. Ten years at the most I intended to stay in America. Life at home would surely have improved in ten years if it was ever going to get better. I thought about my brother Seán who was gone since 1947 without making a visit home in all that time. I wasn't sure that I was doing the right thing because I was drawing my pay in England and it was fairly close to home. Páidí and Máirín were already in America; now we'd all be together. If I wasn't happy there I could go back to England after a year.

It was the neighbours' dog that woke me that Autumn morning, the day that Dónall and I had arranged to hoist our sails and turn our faces to the windy city of Chicago. When I was stretching myself in the bed I thought of the people before me who had left home when I was a child. I barely remember my brother Seán walking down the village boreen to the top of the new road where a car was waiting for him. He wasn't on his own because there were three more young boys from the parish emigrating with him. That same year, our next-door neighbour, Dave Russell, went across the sea. Six or seven years afterwards, my brother Páidí emigrated and the following year, my sister Máirín. The father and mother rear their family and, just when they're reared, off they go out the front door to foreign places, maybe never to return home again. The family heartbroken after them. It doesn't make reason or sense.

I put on my clothes while my mother fried black puddings and bacon over the fire. I hadn't much of an appetite that morning, and Dónall wasn't much better. My mother called us to the table and ordered us to eat a good breakfast because it might be well out in the day before we'd get anything to eat again. I looked south east on Caherscuilibeen Hill that was visible from the kitchen window. My thoughts began to drift again. The Sundays I spent hunting on that hill. I walked to the door and up to the gable of the house. North east of me, Mount Brandon stood majestically. North of me was Brandon Creek, where Saint Brendan sailed from to face the wild sea in search of the new land he saw in his dreams. West of that was Baile Dháith Tower, breaking every storm no matter how strong and giving shelter to the parish.

My mother called me in and told me to put something in my stomach because we had a long day and night ahead of us. To please my mother, I went in and sat at the table. The neighbours came in as they always did when anybody was emigrating from home. My father was sitting in the corner without a word out of him. I felt that he was very quiet. There was the noise of a car approaching.

'Jack Moran is outside,' my mother said hurrying us up. We walked as far as the door.

'Well,' said my father, taking my hand, 'we weren't lonely the last time you left because we didn't know you were going away. Do you know, I'd nearly prefer if ye did the same thing today.'

I went out over the threshold with a lump in my heart. Dónall wasn't far behind me. I didn't look east or west but kept my head down until I was inside in the car. Yes, if we were heartbroken how were the old couple that reared us and were watching us leaving now …

19

It was a four-engine Pan Am plane that took us across to America. We were about twelve hours in the air but we didn't feel it because when we weren't eating, we were watching films. Yes boy! A cinema up in the sky. We were sitting over the wings, and that didn't help things too much. Dónall took out his rosary beads a few times with the fright that was on him. When we were in the air five hours or so we went into a patch of bad weather. 'Turbulence' the pilot called it. Upon my soul I wasn't long strapping myself into the seat when the turbulence started. 'We hit an air pocket,' someone said. Eventually day dawned. Below us was solid ground. I thought about the poet who wrote the song: 'To America west I'll go hunting while still my youth I can count on / Hunting for gold underground by the sides and the edge of the mountain.' I didn't know if any of that gold would come in my direction. It's many a mother's son crossed the Atlantic searching for that same gold and it would have been better for some of them if they had stayed at home because they did no good for themselves or for anyone else either.

'I feel a lot better,' said Dónall 'now that we're over solid ground.'

Without a doubt, I wasn't going to make him any happier.

'I don't know,' I said, 'if the plane is going to crash, I'd prefer to fall into the sea than to have my head stuck a foot into the ground in the middle of Ohio.'

Dónall wasn't too happy with that.

'Yerra,' he said, 'put away that kind of talk. Didn't you often hear that mocking is catching.'

At ten to one the pilot spoke to us through the loudspeakers.

'We're ten minutes from Midway Airport,' he told us. 'Everybody get ready for descent.'

I was looking down at the big, wide city below us. Streets running as straight as a rule from north to south and the same west and east. On the east side of the city as far as you could see was a huge lake. That was Lake Michigan, no doubt, as I found out before too long. We hadn't much of a delay going through customs because we hadn't a lot of baggage. Through the pane of glass we had a view of the people who were waiting outside.

'Do you see any of ours?' asked Dónall, wiping his glasses.

It wasn't long before we saw my sister Máirín and my brother Páidí. Their faces were happy and welcoming before us. As soon as we came through the door, the four of us had our arms around one another. Tears of happiness came to my eyes because we were together again. They gave us both a hearty welcome to America and wished us every luck while we were in that country. They took us out to the car they had brought with them. Dónall was amazed that Páidí had his own car, but Páidí told him that he had it for over a year. It was a fine big car like the Americans have. I was examining it.

'I wouldn't like to be taking it down the Carrachán road,' I said. 'They'd have to widen the crooked bridge. What make is it?' I asked.

We were driving out on the street by this time. I was told that it was a Chevvy and that the only fault it had was that it was very heavy on petrol.

Páidí and Máirín were living on the west side of the city, on the corner of Washington Boulevard and Cicero Avenue. Páidí was married with over a year to a girl from the county Mayo. Mary O'Grady was her name before she married.

'Oh, we heard the good news a week ago. Congratulations,' Dónall said.

I knew that a young daughter was born to the two of them.

'The baptism was this morning,' Páidí told us, reddening a cigarette.

'Look, Dónall, at the length of the cigarettes in this place. Upon my soul, they're six inches long if they're an inch,' I said in amazement.

We reached our destination. 'That's the house over there,' Máirín informed us pointing towards a brick house with two levels.

'We're living on the second level,' Páidí said. We went up the stairs. There was music coming from the apartment when we were getting near it. I asked Páidí who was playing.

'That's a record,' he informed me. 'Some of our friends are coming for dinner, that's a custom in this place'.

Well if you saw the fine apartment. There were three bedrooms in it, a sitting room and a fine roomy kitchen. I prodded Dónall.

'These aren't the poky little rooms we had to live in in England,' I said. 'Not to mention the wall-to-wall carpet.' Dónall answered me.

'Oh my, America is a wealthy place. Thanks be to God. This place looks like it's fairly rich people who're living here.'

We were introduced to the visitors who had come to the house.

'Yes wisha, this is no dry baptism,' I said to Máirín, looking at the table full of bottles.

We were asked would we have a 'shot' as they say over there

and we were given a small glass each. There was no need for him to say any more. We needed a drink after our journey.

'May your hand kill a pig,' I said, knocking it back.

We were given a bottle of beer as well. Some of the people around us were fairly merry and they had all the appearances of having knocked back a bottle or two before this. All the women went into the kitchen and the men were left in the sitting room talking and gossiping and drinking the odd drop. We had no shortage of music because when one record would finish another would drop down on top of it. Your bottle wouldn't be empty when another bottle would be brought out to you from the kitchen and it cooled in the freezer. Páidí's wife called out from the kitchen after a while:

'Dinner is ready.'

Yes, wisha, there was need for a bite by that time. Dónall and I waited till the company were sitting at the table.

'Come on,' said Páidí, beckoning from the door of the kitchen. In the centre of the table was a great lump of roast turkey. If that bird was one pound weight it was surely twenty-five pounds. Don't be talking about the vegetables that came with it. There were two big bowls of pandy, what we call boiled potatoes with butter, as well. There was a big difference between this food and the strips of horse meat we were eating for the past year.

''Tis no wonder,' said Dónall with a big plate of food in front of him, 'that the most of the Yanks have big heads of meat on them.'

We ate food and drank wine until our appetites were satisfied. Then dessert and strong coffee were put in front of us. If a fellow could get a comfortable corner to lie down in, he was made. But that wasn't what was in store for us. Everybody went out into the sitting room again and I was handed an accordion.

'Play us a few tunes,' said my brother Páidí, 'till I see if you've improved any bit.' I did as he asked.

At the end of the evening, the company scattered and I sat around the kitchen table with Máirín, Dónall, Páidí and his wife. Without a doubt there were many questions about this and that. Was such-and-such a man still living and was such-and-such a woman dead?

'This is a deadly place for coffee,' exclaimed Dónall, pouring another cup for himself.

'Listen, Máirín, where's the red fellow?' I enquired.

My brother Seán I was talking about. I was told he was gone to California for a load of oranges. Seán was a lorry driver.

'Yes,' said Páidí, 'and there'll be no shortage of oranges around Tinley Park next week.'

'How's that?' asked Dónall as innocent as a child.

It was explained to him that some of the boxes had a habit of falling off the back of the lorry on the way home.

'Yes,' I said, 'a nod is as good as a wink to a blind man.'

We were asked were we too tired to go out dancing that night. The dance hall was only around the corner from us.

'I'm as fresh as a daisy,' I exclaimed, jumping from my chair.

'I don't know,' Dónall said, 'I didn't get a wink of sleep on the plane last night.'

I told him he wouldn't have been like that if he threw away his beads and knocked back a few jorums of whiskey.

'The best thing ye can do now is lie back in a hot bath and have a good dip for yere bones.'

We did as she said and, do you know, it was as good as four hours' sleep to me.

At nine o'clock everybody was dressed for the dance.

'We'll go to Tommy Naughton's pub for an hour first,' Páidí said when we left the house.

He wanted me to hear a musician called Paddy Doran playing. This place was down in Pulaski Road about a mile or so from the apartment. It was mainly Irish who went in there. Paddy Doran was the man who was serving behind the bar. He gave Páidí a hearty welcome.

'It looks like you're a good customer from the fine welcome you got from that boyo,' said Dónall.

'Maybe I'm here too often at times,' Páidí answered.

We were introduced to Paddy and he put up the first drink.

'Do they stand to you in every pub here when you come in for the first time?' I asked.

'Don't worry,' said Páidí, 'because they'll get it back off of you in the end.' He called Paddy after a while.

'Play a few tunes on the whistle for the greenhorn,' he said.

Anybody who came to America for the first time was called a greenhorn. He was a fine musician. I found out after that he was from the county Leitrim, which was the home of the finest of the flute players. He was told that I was a musician as well. Paddy asked me had I my box and I had to tell him that I hadn't. We promised that we'd give him a visit during the week and bring the accordion with us. Shortly afterwards we said goodbye to the Leitrim man and headed for the dance.

Don't be talking about space. People used to say that the Round Tower in Holloway was big, but if you saw the Keyman's Club you'd say that the Round Tower was only a cabin. I suppose there was in or about a thousand people in there. There were girls there so covered in paint and powder that you'd have to get a shovel to them to find out if they were good looking.

There were girls there without any paint too. They were big and they were small. Every shape and make you could imagine and they clustered together like midges. Máirín called us over to a vacant table she had spotted.

'Oh Máirín, isn't it the grand sight,' I exclaimed.

'What sight?' she enquired.

'Women, women, women,' I replied. She let out a scart of a laugh.

'I'm going to the counter,' Páidí said. 'What'll ye have to drink?'

Everybody ordered a drink and I got a desire to go dancing to the fine music. I caught hold of Máirín and took her out dancing and, if I did, I was giving the odd look at the fine women that were out on the floor. Any man who left that hall on his own had only himself to blame. There was a great band there: Johnny O'Connor's band, we were told.

'Wait till ye hear Timmy Clifford playing for the sets soon,' somebody said.

We were introduced to a lot of people that night. They were there from every county in Ireland, especially Mayo, Kerry and Galway. It seems that there were five such halls in Chicago and every one of them full to the door. The thought that ran into my head when I looked at the crowd was that if emigration continued for a few more years there would be nobody left at home in Ireland only the old people. I went out dancing with a beauty from Galway. I was too tired to get involved with any girl that night, but I promised her I'd be in the hall again the following Friday and she told me she'd be there too. I was fine and happy with that. I said goodbye to her and headed back to the bar. My brother Páidí was there talking to the musician, Timmy Clifford, that I mentioned earlier. After I was introduced to him,

Timmy excused himself and went back up on to the stage. It was no shame for him to go up on the stage with his accordion. He had a north Kerry style of playing and why wouldn't he? Wasn't he from Castleisland?

'Twas well into the morning when Dónall and I got out of the bed the following day. We weren't used to the difference in time between the two sides of the Atlantic and we had a touch of jetlag although we understood nothing about that at the time. When we had eaten a fine hearty breakfast I decided to have a look at the city. There wasn't half as much smoke in this city as there was in London. I was warned not to go walking anywhere that black people were living. The streets in Chicago were fine compared to the crooked, narrow streets of London. Every street in the city was straight and wide. I went on a bus and I decided to go to the end of the line on it. The driver spotted that I wasn't long in Chicago and he gave me a map of all the bus trips a person could make in the city. He was a very friendly man and he wasn't lazy to give me any information I wanted. I asked him about work in the city and he told me that most of the factories were on the south side. But there weren't too many jobs going at this time of year only maybe in Montgomery Ward or Sears Roebuck. He gave me more advice; if I could drive a bus or a lorry I'd have no trouble getting a job. But the bicycle was the biggest machine I had driven up to this! I gave the day examining the city, sometimes on a bus, sometimes walking. I was in no hurry but was observing things. The houses in the city, they were a lot bigger and more spacious than the houses in London. The cars were very plentiful and they were a lot bigger than the cars in England. When I got home that evening I told them that I'd go looking for work in the morning.

'You'd be better off taking it easy, my boy, because you'll be working for the rest of your life,' was the advice I got from Páidí.

I got up early the following morning. I had a few addresses in my pocket, a list of a couple of factories. There was no point in looking for work out in the open air at this time of year as the winter was upon us. The first factory I tried was Western Electric, a mighty big factory. All this trouble to get a job there. I had to fill in a handful of forms, do an interview, be examined by a doctor and still I wasn't offered a job. What they said to me was that they would call me when they needed me. When I asked them when that would be they told me it would be some time before Christmas. That was no good to me. I got out of that place and went to Sears Roebuck because I had heard that they needed workers.

The Sears Roebuck factory was in a black area. It was the same there with forms, but I knew immediately that they were looking for workers. The place was full of black people and they all looking for work too. After I had filled the forms, I was told that I would have to do an exam. I told them that I didn't want an office job but manual work. It was no good. The exam would help me, I was told, if I wanted to get ahead. I had to do the exam and, to tell you the truth, the questions on the papers that were put in front of me weren't too hard. I gave my written answers to some man or other and he studied them. He told me to wait outside in another hall until I was called. I waited for about an hour. I was called in the end and a brown envelope was handed to me. I would have to give this envelope to some doctor who was up on the ninth floor. I was told that I'd have a job if I got on all right with the doctor. How much would I be making here, I enquired. Two dollars and seventy five cents an hour and there would be overtime as well. I was told that when I came in in the morning to go to Mike McRory, that he would be waiting for me if everything was all right with the doctor.

I surprised Dónall when I came back to the house and told him that I had got a job in Sears Roebuck. He would go looking for work there tomorrow. I was told that there had been a telephone call from my brother Seán and he'd be with us at seven o'clock. We'd be all here before him and why wouldn't we? I hadn't seen Seán since 1947 when I was only five years old.

'Yerra, ye're not fledglings any more,' said Seán taking the fill of his eyes from Dónall and me.

We welcomed each other heartily and it was no wonder. We threshed out many a subject that evening. There was nobody from the top of the parish of Moore back to Imlea that wasn't spoken of that night. Seán told stories of his childhood in Ireland and we weren't backward with our own stories either. Not a word of English was spoken that night but the bit we spoke to Páidí's wife. Seán told us that he and his wife had got a new house a fortnight before this. His wife was busy at home putting up the curtains. All the same, we would have to spend the next weekend with them. We didn't find the time going and it was after one o'clock in the morning when we said goodbye to each other.

20

At a quarter to eight the following morning I found Mike McRory in Sears Roebuck. He was a friendly man and the first thing he said to me was:

'How are they all in the cabbage patch?'

When I didn't understand rightly what he meant, he started to laugh. He told me that he was from Donegal himself. He had forty men working under him and four of those were black. When he asked me what I thought about working with black people I told him I didn't mind working with black people or any other race as long as they did their work right. He told a girl to call George Smith. After a while a small black man came in. He was told that I would be working with him.

'Now Mr McRory, some white folk don't like to work with their coloured brethren. You know what happened the last time, man,' said George. Mr McRory put him at his ease and told him that he thought that we'd get along fine.

'Do you mind the colour of my skin?' he asked me.

I told him I didn't. Then McRory got up and told me to go with George and he'd show me what to do. I thought the Irishman had a smirk on his face. Nobody could understand George's accent. I found it hard to understand him and I told him to speak slower. We were working out on the docks and we would have to take goods from the lorries and keep an account of them. There was everything from women's stockings to fridges coming off of those same lorries. We had small four-wheel carts to move the merchandise from place to place. I had no bother getting into the work, even though some of the boxes that were on the lorries were fairly heavy. But I had experience of lifting weighty things in England. We were fiddling around until George called me in for a cup of tea. We weren't allowed to smoke in the place we were working in outside, but there was one room set aside for smoking. The room was full to the door when we went in. George gave me half of his sandwich and I offered him a cigarette. He whispered in my ear and told me to pretend nothing but people were looking at us.

We went out again after the break. When I was going out the door I felt a finger on my shoulder. A man was behind me and he signalled to me that he wanted to have a word in my ear.

'I'll be with you in a couple of seconds,' I said, catching hold of my partner's jacket.

'If I were you,' the man said to me, 'I wouldn't be hanging around with that nigger.'

I broke out in pins and needles from head to foot. Here was a man I had never seen before in my life trying to tell me what to do. I told him without any fear to mind his own business and if I wanted his advice, I'd ask for it. I went out then without saying another word. My partner said nothing.

I got used to the work quickly. When I got to know George rightly I found out that he was a fine, decent misfortune and he was only in this world to make amends for the sins of his ancestors. George liked a drop of gin, music and women. Like he used to say: 'When a black man don't look at ladies and drink gin it is time to call in the undertaker'. Nobody knew about his fluency with words. He was married and divorced twice. 'Between marriages and breaking in a young filly' as he said himself. I could say anything to him. One day I asked him how many times a week would he get a desire for Flori. She was his girlfriend. Three times he told me.

'Aren't you a bit old for that *craic* now?' I said.

He said he wasn't because he was taking nature pills. I never found out what kind of a dose was in those nature pills.

'How do you do the action in the summer when it's hot?' I continued. He had a plan.

'I wake her up at four in the morning when it is nice and cool,' he told me. '"Flori," I says, "it is exercise time."' His two eyes were dancing with roguery.

We were paid at lunchtime every Friday. You could change your cheque at a bank in the factory if you wanted to. Because everybody was fine and happy every Friday evening with money in their pockets, the *craic* would be thick and heavy. My partner wasn't far behind. One evening he told me a story about himself and Flori. They were going out with each other for a while and he made a date with her outside a 'gin mill' as he called it. Not long before that a new fashion came out in ladies' dresses. The wider the dress the more it was in fashion. The dresses would remind you of nothing, said George, but dresses women wear when they are pregnant. 'Moo, moo dresses' I think they were called. When he met Flori that night, she was wearing one of those dresses. He examined her well.

'Flori, is you in style or is I in trouble?' he said. That's how George told the story.

I didn't find the time going until we were into November. It was then the work started in earnest for Christmas. The traffic coming in got bigger and, of course, so did the traffic going out. Often we were unloading lorries until midnight just before Christmas. When work was over for the day I had to make my own way home on the bus. Many's the time my heart was in my mouth waiting for the bus because, as I already said, the Sears Roebuck factory was in a black area. I often saw them on my way home and they throwing a dirty eye at me. I was walking the streets at night with my two fists closed in case I'd be attacked. Unemployment, alcoholism and even drugs were prevalent in that area. Even if George was going in my direction – maybe they wouldn't interfere with me if there was a black man with me. When I said as much to George one morning, he started laughing. 'Twas all the one if you were black, yellow or white, he said, if you had something in the bottom of your pocket. It was the way that the black people were getting impatient because they weren't getting fair treatment from the white man. Some of the blacks were educated now and they understood things better. They understood how the black race were made slaves at first and now they were looking for civil rights and jobs. But their demands were falling on deaf ears. The young people were going around making trouble. I often heard of attacks on people that I knew.

'Listen,' said George, 'things are only beginning. Unless the politicians and employers change their minds, blood will be spilled yet.'

I had to agree with him when I looked around me. There were only three black people working in the corner I was working in and two of those were sweeping the floor. There were more than sixty white men there and this was in a black area. As I heard it, it was the same with every company. But I had enough responsibilities of my own without being too concerned about other people's troubles. All the same I wasn't too happy about the black man's lot. George often told me about his people's music and customs and I got great pleasure from his stories. I often thought, too, about the way our own race was persecuted.

Many nationalities were working in Sears. They were from Poland, Italy, and the Jew was there as well. Another crowd that was there were the Hillbillies, people from places like Tennessee and Alabama who didn't have much education. Even though there was that mixture of people there, they got on with one another. Maybe there might be the odd argument but I never saw anybody using their fists.

Shortly before Christmas, Mike McRory called me into his office and told me that the company was very satisfied with me and maybe I'd be made permanent after Christmas. Maybe, however, I'd be transferred to some other department.

It was a mail-order plant we were in, and, just before Christmas, the orders started slowing down because there was no point in ordering through the post too close to Christmas for fear that the order wouldn't arrive. The company had a shop as well but our section only dealt with orders through the post. Sears Roebuck had seven hundred shops all over America and, when I say shops, I don't mean Katie Sarah's shop in Dingle. But when the orders slowed down just before Christmas, the work wasn't there and they were letting people go. When I came in people were being hired as thickly as flies but now they had to leave again. Thanks be to God I had a promise that I would be kept on. I often saw five or six outside the door of the office and it was no good news the man in the office had for them.

Three days before Christmas, McRory called me into his office.

'I told you earlier,' he began, 'that maybe we'd find you another position in the company. Not because you're Irish but because you are open-minded and we need people like you in our company.'

I was told to go to another department to a black man called

Mr Wall and he'd fix me up. Yes, I'd have no need to be going around looking for work for another while anyway. It doesn't cost you anything to be civil to people.

21

Since I always had an interest in music, I went around the city listening to various musicians. There were a couple of hours of Irish music and song on the radio every Saturday morning. As well as the music, they used to give out information on the programme about where the sessions, the commotion and the *craic* were taking place. I found it hard at times to make up my mind about which place to go to for music, there were so many of them. But there was one place I used to go to more than the rest every Sunday. That was Hanley's Pub on the south side of the city. It was the biggest Irish pub in Chicago. I went there the first time with my brother Seán. 'Hanley's House of Happiness' was written over the door. There were ten men working behind a counter that was fifty yards long.

If there was one person in the bar there were three hundred. Right in front of the counter there was a dance floor and at the top of the house was a stage. We weren't long there that first night when two men came up to us. One man saluted Seán in lovely, sweet Irish. 'We didn't see you with years,' one of them said to him. Seán told him that he wasn't living in Chicago itself any more but that he had a house a bit outside the city. Then Seán introduced the two men to me. They were Fitzgeralds from Baile Uachtarach. They left Ireland before I began my travels. Tom Fitzgerald was getting impatient when the music wasn't starting. He didn't have long to wait, however, because when we looked over there were six musicians sitting at the one table. They were all getting their instruments ready and tuning them.

'Look at the man with the wavy hair and he going bald in front,' Seán told me. 'His name is Joe Cooley. He's as good a musician as ever left Ireland. Sitting beside him is his brother Séamus with a wooden flute in his hand. They came over with the Tulla Céilí Band six or seven years ago and they stayed here after them.'

No sooner had he spoken than the music started up and, if it did, everybody stopped talking. I thought when I was in England that I saw musicians whose betters I'd never see but if I ever saw six skilled musicians playing together they were in Hanley's pub that Sunday night. Joe Cooley was there with a fag between his lips, his fingers spinning through every tune. His head was thrown back and his heart and mind were immersed in the music. Among the musicians was a man called Mike Neary. He was a middle-aged man with a sweet style on the fiddle. His sister Eleanor was there and she was a famous piano player. I was listening to Seán naming them and I was trying hard to bring the music with me at the same time. On the drums was Billy Soden, a man who also came over with a band. Then another man sat down in their company. Seán told me that he was Kevin Keegan, a man who had played with the Aughrim Slopes Céilí Band up to shortly before that. When he was in right form, he'd knock smoke out of a lot of musicians. There were two brothers from south Galway in the band, Bertie and Tom McMahon, one of them on the banjo and the other on the fiddle. Now if I could count all the musicians, there were at least twenty-five of them there in the pub that evening. Any one of them would have got his place in any band in Ireland they were such good musicians. It was there the music was at that time and not in Ireland. Isn't it a strange world, the best of musicians and every mother's son of them had to turn his back on his native land. There wasn't the same thought of Irish music and culture in Ireland as there was in America. Musicians in Chicago were making good money. You could be playing in Ireland from one end of the week to the next and all you'd get for your work was, 'God spare you the health'.

They gave the whole night playing reels and jigs. What was going through my head was where did they get all the fine tunes? They played four or five tunes one after the other for half an hour or so. Shortly after that, six or seven other musicians were pressed into the music. Even though the musicians came from different parts of Ireland and some were born in America they were able to play with one another no bother at all. If one of them had to play a solo, it's in his own county's style he would play. When I asked Joe Cooley about this one time, what he had to say was that everybody had to make concessions to everybody's else's style when a group was playing. 'Neutral ground' he called it. Out into the night, Seán prodded me. He told me to bring in my own box. I said I wouldn't because I'd prefer to listen and maybe I'd learn something. But all he did was to go over to Joe Cooley and whisper in his ear. It wasn't long after that I saw Cooley coming over to me and offering me his box. After the fine music that was played what would a person do? I put my mind to two slides I had learned in England from a man who hailed from Castleisland.

'Up Cuas!' It was from the middle of the floor the shout came. Tom Fitzgerald it was who was there prancing around the floor to the music. I played a few easy jigs then and soon a couple of musicians fell in with me. I knew from Cooley's box that it was on the same note as my own and I had no difficulty with it. After a few more tunes I put away the box. Joe Cooley pulled me back.

'There's a radio programme being made immediately. Maybe you'd play two slides because there's nothing like a fresh musician,' he said.

A woman who was sitting near Cooley asked him what was the name of the last tune I played. He looked at me and roguery written across his face.

'O, love, I haven't a name on any tune,' I said.

But Cooley wasn't long getting a name for it. 'Mary Hold the Candle till I Shave the Gander's Leg': That's the name that Cooley himself put on it. Of course the woman who asked the question didn't know any better. Then he took up the accordion and started playing with a face as innocent as a baby on him. Every Sunday without fail I paid a visit to Hanley's pub. I got very friendly with the Cooley brothers. Nobody knows how many tunes I got from them and many's the funny story Joe told me because he was a right comedian. He always said that its own misfortune followed music.

'Drink follows music and, if you take my advice, stay away from the whiskey because it will put a shake in your hand and it will scatter your mind. 'Twas that same music put many a healthy man astray,' he used to say.

There was one rule in Hanley's pub. Any musician who played there got plenty of drink. A glass of whiskey and a bottle of beer was the regular drink there. Without a doubt, when you'd have a couple of those knocked back every drink after that would go down easily. Everything would be fine until the alarm clock rang the following morning. I was lucky in a way because I would only go to the south side of the city once a week. But most of the Irish who were living on that side of the city, it's to Hanley's they would go on their way home from work in the evenings. Drink is a bad supper. Any get-together or party the Cooleys couldn't play for, they put the job my way. After a while I was fairly busy with the box. One evening after work and I stretching myself in the bath, my sister Máirín said to me that there was a telephone call for me. A man by the name of Bill Sullivan was on the phone. He told me that he had a pub on Chicago Avenue, a place that was within an ass's roar of where I was living. He said that he was looking for a musician for every Saturday night and that he got my name from Joe Cooley. We discussed money and when I was offered sixty dollars a night, upon my soul, I had nothing to ask him but what time of the night would I be playing. I was told I would be playing from ten o'clock till three o'clock in the morning and that I'd have a microphone to help me. By God, but everything was going right for me. Along with my weekly pay I would have at least sixty dollars on top of that. I'd have no bother playing Saturday nights because I'd have the Sunday free from work. The first visit a person makes to a place is the hardest, they say. That's how I was the first Saturday night I went to Sullivan's pub. Bill was a big, handsome man and you'd have no need to ask him what part of Ireland he came from because as soon as he opened his mouth you'd know his Carrantouhill accent. He stood me a drink after welcoming me. Then he showed me where I'd be playing. He'd send up a couple of singers during the night to give me a break from playing.

'It's a Clare, Galway and Kerry crowd that mostly come in here,' he told me. 'They like fine fast music.'

I didn't exert myself too much at first but played one tune after the other. By the time midnight came there was a good crowd gathered and some of them wanted to dance. An old fellow came up to me after a while and he told me that the man of the house sent him up to sing. I wasn't long handing him the microphone. I often heard worse singers and I often heard better. One thing that ran into my head when I heard the same man was that there were at least forty verses in his song if there was one. It gave me a good chance to go to the counter to get a drink and I was back again and halfway down my glass and the song wasn't still finished. At half past one, a young crowd came in after the dance. I saw a lot of my companions among them. There were a couple of tradesmen from Castleisland there and they were fairly merry.

'Play a set,' said Mike Scollard who was among them.

He was a man I got to know the first week I came to Chicago. Eight went out dancing and it wasn't long before they rose the dust from the floor. I looked over at the man of the house. He was filling drink as fast as he could with a fine satisfied look on him.

22

Every weekend I had the habit of following a pattern I laid down for myself. For instance, I'd go to the dance every Friday night in the Keyman's Club near us. Making money was what was bothering me every Saturday night. I'd head for the south side of the city early every Sunday evening. I'd be depending on some friend or other to give me a drive home and, if that failed, I'd have to use public transport. A man I got to know shortly after coming to Chicago was Mike Scollard. He was from Glaunthane near Castleisland. He was a great character full of harmless tricks and roguery. He came to Chicago about the same time as myself. He was a great talker and he put it to good use because within a month in the city he had a job in Midway Airport working for United Airlines. A job any Irish-man would give his right hand for. He was earning in or about three hundred dollars a week and at that time a labouring man was only earning about half that amount. It was no wonder, so, that he got a car without delay. Any place he was going at the weekends, he'd let me know. If I happened to be going to the same place, he'd be outside the door to give me a drive. He was a big-hearted man who would help any of his friends. He was a fine, sweet singer too. He had a lot of old ballads in English and, when he had a drop taken, he'd burst into song inside in the middle of a church.

When he came to Chicago first he came with a girl he was very fond of at home. Without going too deeply into the story, she wasn't long going with another man when she found herself in Chicago and she left Mike without any explanation. Overnight she was married to some Hillbilly. Mike started drinking then and he often told me that he didn't care what shape he'd be in because his heart was broken. All his friends were trying to advise him but he didn't listen to them. He had no desire to go to dances and, even when he did, he had no desire to go and talk to any girl. He'd spend the whole night at the bar.

'Listen, Mike Scollard,' I used to say to him, 'do you think you are causing her any worry? Put her out of your head and look around you. They're in front of your eyes, fine, handsome girls and they taking the heels off of one another to have a date with you.'

He often visited me in the apartment in the middle of the week and I make out that all he wanted was someone to talk to. He had no desire to go to the Keyman's Club because he'd meet too many of his people from home.

'Yerra,' I used to say to him, 'aren't there a couple of halls on the south side of the city and another one on the north side?'

At long last he gave in to me a little and changed his ways. After a while he put the sadness and sorrows of life completely behind him and he went out in company again. I think that when I mentioned the other halls in the city that he put it before him to go to the south side every Friday instead of going to the Keyman's Club. He came to me one Friday night. He was clean, shaved, washed and had a new suit of clothes on him. When I looked at him, I knew well that he was coming to himself.

'Would you say now,' he said with a fine satisfied air, 'that there's some girl who'd give me the love of her heart?'

I told him that they'd be taking the heels off of one another coming to him. We went south. When we reached the hall there was a good crowd gathered there already. We went as far as the bar to have one bottle while we were looking around. He told me to come to him if I met a nice girl and wanted to take her home. He would take us anywhere in the city in his car. We weren't long inside when Mike told me that he was going out dancing and he left me. I stayed at the counter observing things and drinking my bottle of beer. Someone thumped me on the back and, when I looked around, who should be there before me but an old friend from my days in Dingle Tech, Jim Choráilí Ó Beaglaoi from Ballydavid. We greeted each other and started to talk about home and the things that happened to us when we were going to school.

Mike came back after a while and, if he did, something was bothering him. He was after seeing a beautiful girl but she wasn't on her own, he told us. We thought that he was talking about a man at first, but he wasn't. It was another girl, her next-door neighbour, that was with her. By God, if 'twas help he wanted, he'd get it. A slow foxtrot stared and we decided that this was the right time to take the two girls out dancing. Mike showed me where the two girls were and I let him go ahead of me so that he could get the girl he wanted. I took the other girl out dancing with me. The girl who was dancing with me was a Costello and her great-grandfather was from Cork. She told me she saw me in the Keyman's Club the first night I was there. I thought about the advice Dainín gave me one time: that was to stay with my own people and not to marry a woman who was born in America. According to him, an American woman wouldn't be long putting an apron on the man she married and not only that but that he'd have to get up in the middle of the night if any of the children started crying. The eyes she was putting through me were making me uncomfortable.

When the dance was over we went back to the bar and Mike was there before us with the other girl on his arm. We had a drink and the girls had two highballs. I noticed that Mike's girl was really lying into him and the girl I had wasn't too far behind her with me.

Mike whispered to me in my ear: 'Jeannie's family are full of money.'

Jeannie was the girl who was dancing with me. I knew that Mike wasn't out for the good of my health. I had to tell my girl that I hadn't any car but there was no fear but that Mike would give us a drive home in his car. We hit the road before the last dance. Mike's excuse was that there was a long road before us on our way home. I knew well what roads he had in his head. We headed north, Mike driving and Theresa almost on his lap. I was in the back seat… I won't say any more about that!

When we reached the place where the girls were living, Jeannie invited us in to her own house so that we could drink tea together.

'Tea!' said Mike. 'Take in Mike O' Shea, girl, and make tea for him. Theresa will make tea for me.' It was no good to be arguing with him.

Then Theresa spoke: 'If we all went into the one house you wouldn't think of going home until morning.'

When he was going away from us into the other house, Mike shouted at me that he would leave the door of the car open in case he'd be late.

'And don't be in any hurry yourself,' he said when he was going in the door with his arm tightly around Theresa.

When we went in, Jeannie gave me a bottle of beer and told me to get a glass for myself in the cupboard. She started clattering with kettles and saucepans. I'd say she did that on purpose for soon I heard the clip-clop coming down the stairs. There was someone else in the house and he was awake.

'Is that you, Jeannie baby?' said a voice.

'Yes, Daddy dear,' she replied, 'come and meet my boyfriend.'

On the spot, I thought of Dainín's advice. Yes, 'boyfriend' and I not having the first move made yet. An old, thin person with a tormented look came in and sat opposite us at the table. He started blinding me with questions about my family and everything about them. I can tell you that I was good enough for him and he didn't hear much of the truth from me. If I caught Mike Scollard now, I'd give him a good shaking because he was responsible for the whole thing. Jeannie came out herself after a while with a cup of tea and a plate full of food. She put a sweet cake in the middle of the table. To tell the truth, I had no desire for tea or food or anything else by this time. I started to drink a sup of tea and to pick at the food.

An hour went by and the old man had no notion of going for the stairs. Oh Holy Mary! If I was married to her and having to put up with the old man and he there in front of me with his pyjamas and slippers every night. Yes, either he or I would go because the street wouldn't be wide enough for the two of us. I looked at my watch.

'Oh my, look at the time,' I said.

'Ah, take it easy,' Jeannie said. 'Dad, go to sleep now,' she told him. He wasn't too happy.

'Will you be all right, Jeannie child?' he asked her.

You'd think by him that I was Jack the Ripper. I headed for the front door but, if I did, she followed me. She cornered me near the door.

'Take it easy,' she said. 'He'll be asleep in a minute.'

But I had every excuse under the sun. If I got my two legs

out on to the street, 'twould be hard to entice me into that house again. She wanted me to phone her during the week and she wrote down the number for me. 'Twould be as well for her to be idle for she'd have a long wait for a phone call from me.

I got to the car at last. Without a doubt there was no trace of Mike Scollard. I made the sign of the cross on my forehead after I had closed the door of the car. I stretched out on the back seat and put my two hands behind my head as if I had a pillow...

'Wake up! I nearly went to Jeannie's house searching for you.' It was Mike Scollard who had come back from the other house. I raised myself up in the seat and yawned. Yes, Casanova had come back from his den. His hair looked like a gale of wind or something like it had caught it.

'If your mother saw you now,' I said to him, handing him a comb that was in my back pocket. 'The fear of the devil must have caught you.' Mike was greatly amused at that.

'I'm coming down again in the middle of the week,' he told me. 'How did you get on?' he enquired. I had to give him some answer.

'The old lad got up and he gave me an oral examination,' I told him. 'I drank a sup of tea and, by the time he was finished with the questions, the wind was gone from my sails. Mike Scollard, I was never in as bad a corner in my life.'

I let on then that I was giving him a tongue-lashing because he was the whole cause of it. But 'twould be as well for me to be idle because he was fattening on the story. When I had said my last, he started the engine of the car.

'All part of your education, my son,' he said as he drove through the city.

23

When a friend of mine by the name of Frank O'Donnell and I were talking one night in Val Connolly's pub, what we were discussing was the effect of overtime on a person's body. Frank was a fine, steady man who would have a drink with any man and wouldn't interfere with anybody. He was working in construction from the first day he came to Chicago.

'I think,' he said, putting his glass down on the counter, 'that anyone who works more than forty hours a week in any job is out of his mind because Uncle Sam takes half his earnings in tax. You have the right plan, Mike, a night here and there with your accordion and doing other small jobs during the week.'

Frank was working twelve hours a day and a half day on Saturday as well.

'I'll tell you the truth, Frank,' I said, 'I didn't take two days' holidays one after the other since I came to Chicago. There's a fortnight coming to me now and I'm thinking of going some place for a week at least to have a little break for myself.' Frank didn't have a holiday for two years he told me.

'Do you know what we'll do?' said Frank. 'We'll head off to some place that's miles away from Chicago.'

'What's been in my head for a while now is that it would be nice to do a tour of the southern states and to find out how the country people live. I'm sick of being stuck in the middle of the city and I half trampled by people,' I said. Frank gave a couple of seconds thinking.

'Maybe there's something in what you've said,' he ventured.

'I was never south of Indiana and it would be no harm to open up the car a bit.'

Frank would be ready for the road on Monday but I had made no arrangements. I'd have to arrange it with the company first and Frank asked me to ring him on the Monday night.

'I'll contact my brother Seán,' I offered, 'he knows every main road from Chicago to the Mexican border because he travels them all around the year. I'll tell him to map out a route for us.'

Shortly after I got to work on Monday morning, I faced the office in Sears Roebuck. I went in and asked for a fortnight's holiday starting the following Monday. I thought that it would be hard to get holidays at such short notice, but I had no trouble at all. I had the bad luck when I was talking to one of my co-workers, Jim Crofton, during the day of telling him where I was going the following week. I was questioning him really because he was from Alabama himself. I showed him the route my brother Seán had mapped out for me on a piece of paper.

'You'll be passing within a couple of miles of my home place,' he informed me. 'I'll give you the address. You'll get a gallon of hooch from them for me. I hadn't a proper drink with four years since I came to this city. I promise you, you won't be left go home dry either. Tell them that Little Jim told you to look them up'.

I looked at my man and he was three or four inches with six feet.

'Oh yes,' he said, 'and don't forget to give my little sister a kiss for me.'

That was one thing I would do, if I was in that boat.

It was the alarm clock jumping on the side of the cupboard that woke me the following Monday morning.

'Turn off that devil of an alarm,' said my brother Dónall, 'or do you want to wake up the whole neighbourhood?'

He didn't have to get up until eleven o'clock because he was working in the shoe department in the same company as me. I threw myself out of the bed at half past six and I knew that Frank wouldn't be late. I boiled the kettle and put an egg into it. That was the breakfast I had nearly every morning because I never liked the frying pan during the week, especially after rising early in the morning. We hit the road at half past seven as we had arranged. It was going into the city most of the traffic was at that time of the morning and because of that we had no trouble getting out of it. Of course our spirits were high.

'Where will we stay tonight?' Frank asked after singing two verses of 'The Cliffs of Dooneen'. I opened the map of the route Seán had made for me and looked at the first town he had marked.

'St Louis, Missouri,' I said. 'I'd say we'll be there fine and early in the evening at our ease.'

There was a big difference between the road we were travelling and the road between Dingle and Tralee. It was as straight as a rule as far as you could see and on each side of us there were huge fields of wheat and corn. There was no hill or hillock to be seen, but rich, flat land and you'd think it was levelled by some giant machine.

'I'd prefer to be looking at the Cliffs of Moher,' Frank exclaimed after we had been travelling for two hours.

You'd think we were making no progress such were the huge fields without a briar or furze bush to be seen. Big ramshackle wooden houses and no smoke rising out of any chimney. As we went further south, the towns got scarcer. The hunger hit us out in the day and we said we'd stop at a restaurant on the side of the road. I noticed that there was a big change in the people's accents already and the girl who was serving us had a fine drawl as had some of the people at the other tables. We headed off again at our ease and I giving the odd look at the map. As we were going further south, the land was getting worse and many of the farms looked like they were abandoned. Then suddenly you'd see a huge holding and a mansion of a house built in the middle of it. It was mostly dry stock that was to be seen and they every age from the yearling calf to the animals that were suitable for the butcher's knife.

We were keeping an eye on road signs. 'We're about a hundred miles from St Louis,' I said to Frank.

'Holy Mary, we had no delay. We'll be there before three. We'll get a place to stay first and then we'll give a ramble around the city.'

The following day we went into Hillbilly country. I'd say that half of the houses were abandoned.

'Who said that Ireland was poor?' Frank commented when he saw an old man on the side of the road and the two knees coming out through his trousers. We passed one dwelling house and there was a sow rooting in the garden. It brought me back to the old sow my next-door neighbour, Tom Horgan, had long ago.

'We'll go to a nice, quiet pub tonight,' said Frank, 'and we'll go to bed early.'

We got a B&B a small bit outside Memphis, Tennessee. There was a pub in the B&B also. The woman of the house put a fine, generous supper in front of us.

'Yes, I have more courage now,' said Frank, sitting down to the table. We ate everything she put on the plate in front of us. She was encouraging us to have extra, but we had more than enough on our plates. We took a nap after our meal and then we went into the pub attached to the B&B. There were only six sitting at the bar. The place had a nice, clean appearance; a wooden floor and the look of a country pub. We started talking to a couple of the locals who were sitting near us. It was my opinion after spending a while talking to them that they were honest, decent people without any worldly wealth. One thing I didn't like about them, though, was that they showed a terrible hatred for the black people. As I had done many times before, I started asking the people at the bar were they giving fair play to the blacks.

'Oh we are,' said one man with a look of mockery on his face. 'When they travel on the bus we put those animals at the back'.

I started to ask them then about local customs and where their ancestors came from. There were quite a lot of Irish among them, they said, people who were working on the railroads long ago and who settled in the area and their descendants were there now. That was easily understood from the surnames some of them had. Out in the night, there was a nice crowd gathered in the bar and strong Hillbilly accents to be heard on every side of us. Only that I was used to hearing them in Sears Roebuck, I would never have understood them, I think, because they had certain words that were never written in any English dictionary. A big stout lump of a man sat down beside us. A big hat on him, a silver star on his shirt and a gun hanging from his side.

'Hello Sam,' he said to the man who was sitting on the other side of him.

'Hello Sheriff,' said the man.

He reminded me of nothing but something I saw in the old cowboy pictures. The man of the house put a glass in front of him and filled it up with whiskey. He took the glass and knocked back the whiskey in one go without ever grimacing. You'd think he had shares in the pub because he made no attempt to pay for any drink he got.

'There's no danger that this place will be raided,' said Frank, looking at your man.

The more he drank, the more talkative he got. From what I could understand of his speech, there was some trouble between white and black youths somewhere in Memphis the previous day. It seems that an eighteen-year-old boy was killed during the incident – one of the blacks. The sheriff hadn't a good word to say about the 'niggers' as he called them. He was blaming the government for the present disorder. He said that they were giving free money to the blacks and they were bone idle. After a while the man who was beside him got a chance to put a word in.

'How did you deal with the nigger who was killed yesterday morning?' he asked.

'A call came to the office that there was trouble to the south of us,' the sheriff began. 'Me and my deputy went in the squad car and when we reached the back street where the fight was there was nobody to be seen but the body of a young black man face down in the middle of the street. I put my boot under his belly and turned him over. There were ten bullets in his body.'

'Don't you have to have an inquest on every body now?' said the other man.

'Oh yes, we have to and I did,' the sheriff replied. 'I told the deputy who was with me to take out his notebook. I looked down at the body. This is the result of the inquest: "The worst case of suicide I have seen in my twenty-five years in the force."' You'd hear the two laughing outside the door.

'Oh, Holy Mary,' said Frank, 'didn't God give the black people a hard cross to bear. Come on to bed, Mike boy, while we still have our health.'

24

We got as far as Birmingham, Alabama well out into the following evening. The countryside had a fairly poor appearance from the time we left Memphis until we reached Birmingham.

'It is said that there are people in this State who never saw a radio or a television,' I remarked.

'There are, wisha,' said Frank, 'and people in this place who never saw a basin of water either.'

He was right because some of the people looked like they never washed their faces since the day they were born. If you saw the old cars some of them had while they looked suspiciously at any strangers going by. From the moment I pulled into this place a kind of a change came over my mind.

'I don't think I'd like to spend the night in this town. I have an address that I got from Jim Crofton, a Hillbilly who works with me,' I said.

There were eighty miles ahead of us but one thing we didn't know was that our journey was to be all over back roads. A lot worse than any road in Ireland. There were no road signs to be seen. Twenty times we thought we had gone astray. We put questions to the odd person we came across but it was hard to get an answer out of them. They looked at us suspiciously and put a few questions themselves before they'd give us any information. After we were travelling a long time we came on a one-horse town with a weather-beaten appearance. One pub in it and a grocer's shop. We decided to have a bottle of beer to wet our throats after the journey. We'd have to get directions, as well, if we were to go to the Croftons. There wasn't a Christian in the pub but ourselves and the man of the house. Frank looked at the state of the place and he looked at me. He asked for two bottles of beer. The beer was as warm as the weather outside. We started talking to the man of the house and we told him our story. He gave us directions because he knew the family of my partner in Sears Roebuck well. It didn't take us long to reach their place because there was only the one side road and the one house. It was a wooden house that had no shape or make to it. An old jeep outside it and it looked like a lick of paint wouldn't do it any harm. Frank knocked at the door but he got no answer. I thought that I saw somebody through the window moving inside when we were driving up to the house. Frank knocked harder a second time. The door opened half a foot. The barrel of a gun came out of it and it was put up against Frank's nose.

'Oh, God forgive me my sins,' Frank said and he the colour of death. 'Nobody knows where he'll die and God forbid that it's here where our parents wouldn't have trace nor tidings of us ever.'

An old man came out with the gun still pointing at Frank.

'Are you revenuers?' he asked.

I started to talk then. I told him quickly that I was working with 'Little Jim' in Chicago. When he heard that he put down the gun and opened the door. He explained to us why they had to be so careful. The revenuers, that is the lawmen, were always after them because they were making hooch illegally. There was an open fire in the house and the woman of the house was cooking on it. There was a young, handsome girl helping her. After they had welcomed us they put us sitting at the table. The man of the house put two mugs in front of us. He took a big earthenware jug down from the top of the cupboard and he let out a fine splash from it into our mugs.

'This is the finest drop that's made in these parts,' the old fellow said.

'O, by the way, "Little Jim" told us to bring him a gallon of the stuff to Chicago,' I said.

'Upon my soul, he didn't lose the taste for it in four years,' exclaimed the old fellow.

I drank a slug from the mug. No sooner had I done it than I had to spit it out again because of the burning I got from it. But a small drop escaped down my throat and went with my breath. I felt the stuff running down through my body to the tips of my toes burning all before it. Frank took a slug from his own mug and, if he did, I noticed that he was changing colour.

'The first slug is the worst,' said the old fellow. 'You won't find it going down for the rest of the evening.'

A young man came in the door. A tall, thin, strapping fellow.

'This is my son Ralph,' the old fellow informed us. 'There's no revenuer in the State of Alabama that wouldn't run a mile from him. He'd shoot the eye out of a crow at three hundred yards while that crow was flying through the air.'

We shook hands with him. He saluted us dryly. We found out that Joshua was the father's name and Lena was the young girl's. Frank and I couldn't keep our eyes off her and, upon my soul, she was putting her eyes through us as well. Looking around the house, you'd know that they weren't rich but all the same it was nice and clean.

'You will stay here tonight. We have an empty room,' said Joshua. I told him that we'd prefer to be going north a bit. He let out another drop of the hard stuff for us and this time he let out a drop for himself and for his son.

'Yerra, what's our hurry north?' said Frank, taking another slug out of the mug and at the same time putting his eye on the young girl.

'Put your two eyes back in your head, my good boy,' I whispered to him, 'or have you forgotten the gun that was at your nose ten minutes ago? If you mess with a girl around here, the custom in this part of the country is to put a gun to the back of your head and march you and the girl up to the altar.'

The women were told to get a bite of food for us. The mother was a very quiet woman who didn't open her mouth since we came into the house. She had all the appearances of having gone through the hardships of life. The hooch was going down better now and, like the old fellow said, we weren't on fire as much after we had knocked back the first drop. I finished the second mug and felt nice and merry after it. It wasn't long before the food was put before us. A black pot in the middle of the table and some mixture in it that I'd never seen before. Hanging from the side of the pot was a big spoon that was used for filling the plates. It wasn't long before the old fellow filled his own plate.

'Here you are, boys, spoon it out for yourselves,' he said, giving the spoon to Frank. Frank put a good dollop on his plate and I did the same. I saw a big cake of bread on the table. The old fellow caught it and tore a big lump out of it with his hands. The son didn't use the spoon at all only caught the pot, turned it on its side and let the food out on his plate. We ate our bellies full and drank the hard stuff that was in our mugs.

'That was the tastiest meal I ever ate,' said Frank, rubbing his belly. We thanked the women who got the meal for us. Frank didn't stop but kept putting his eyes through the young girl. The jug was taken down again.

'Yes, boys, have another drop and it will clean your throats,' said Joshua, letting out another jorum to every one of us except the women. Upon my soul but we didn't refuse him this time because you could say that we were getting fond of it. We gave a while talking and in the end the old fellow got up.

'Come with us,' he said, 'we'll go to the saloon. We'll take the old lorry because I'm taking a barrel of "white mule" there.' Frank advised me to bring the accordion with me.

'Have you a musical instrument with you?' asked Ralph who didn't open his mouth since he said 'howdy' to us when he came in first.

Frank and I were put sitting in the front of the old truck with the old fellow and the girl behind us, a barrel of hooch between them in a big wooden box. The son was driving – if you could call it driving. There was gravel and dust rising up from the back wheels of the lorry and the young man with his shoe to the floor. Even though the road was in a dreadful condition, it didn't take us long to reach a small town that was four miles away.

'This isn't the way we came,' said Frank and he throwing his eyes around this weather-beaten old town. It was mainly wooden buildings that were in this town and the houses looked like it was many a day since they got a rub of a paintbrush and there was an odd house here and there missing a plank or two. My man pulled the truck up in front of a big old ramshackle of a wooden house. You'd often see that kind of saloon in the old films.

'By the devil,' said Frank, who had the appearance that the hooch was working on him, 'you'd think that you should see Wyatt Earp walking in through the door with Doc Holliday behind him and two guns hanging off of the both of them.'

We let the Croftons in before us and after we had followed them in I started looking around me. Near the counter there were five or six old fellows sitting, one or two of them chewing tobacco and the juice going down the sides of their mouths. A strong, stale smell of beer and smoke in the place and a look on the floor that it hadn't been swept for a week. Frank asked us what we'd have to drink and he put a twenty dollar bill down on the counter. If you saw the looking the old fellows had at that bill. One fellow almost swallowed the tobacco he was chewing with the start he got. I whispered to Frank that he should stand to the old fellows as well. I didn't have to tell him a second time. We drank a couple of drinks together and Frank and I were fairly well on after the hooch we drank in the house and the drinks we were drinking here. We were drinking and talking until well out in the night. An old fellow who had a hat with a hole in it pulled out a fiddle and he knocked sparks out of it. Then the sport and gaiety started. It was wonderful music. That kind of music is called bluegrass. The man who was serving us got a Jew's Harp and he fell in playing music with the man on the fiddle.

'Now,' said Frank, who had two fine red eyes on him by this time and he sitting beside the young girl of the Croftons, 'that's fine music not like the ould clattering you make on your box, Mike O'Shea.' He had a fine grin on his face.

'Give me the jug,' said the old fellow who was in our company. Maybe you saw the earthenware vessels the whiskey used to come in long ago. He caught one of those and started blowing into the hole at the top and he brought out a kind of music from it. Soon I saw Frank putting his hand up to his eye and he was picking at it as if a fly or something like that was after going into it.

'What's wrong with you?' I enquired.

'A bit of tobacco from the man playing the jug that came into my eye,' Frank said, 'and I can tell you that it's crucifying me'.

Some more people came in during the evening and we noticed that they weren't mixing with us at all. I asked Ralph why they weren't coming into our company. He told me that they were Hillbillies and the crowd who came in were River Rats. I asked him about these River Rats. It appears that they came from the banks of the Mississippi when the Civil War was on between the North and the South. They helped the Yankees and betrayed Lee's army. When Ralph had said that much he let a spit out of his mouth that would hang wallpaper for you. I found that my head was getting light by the end of the night and, as for Frank, he was no better than a dummy and the devil was still trying his luck with the girl. I got a desire to piss which was no wonder after all I had knocked back, not to mention the hooch. I asked them where was the toilet and I was directed out the back door behind the house. I knew what I was doing although my legs were fairly unsteady by this time. There wasn't much of a toilet outside, only a long, white wall and it tarred at the bottom. I had a hard enough job to open my buttons but, in the end, I was able to do my business and immediately there was a fine, healthy stream and it went with the fall. Oh, I felt the relief already. When I thought it was time for it to be running dry, it was rising the stream was. If I was a minute there with the stream going with the fall, I was twenty minutes.

'Holy Mary,' I said, 'I wonder was it that damned hooch that burned out some washer in me and now I can't stop?'

I heard a noise. 'Mike O'Shea,' it said, 'are you after falling into some hole? You're gone with half an hour.' It was Frank that was looking for me.

'I'm all right,' I told him, 'that stuff we were drinking has a hole burned right down through me.' He walked over to me.

'Shame on you, you stump of a fool. Turn off that water tap that's flowing against the wall,' Frank said, and he in stitches laughing.

'Well, thanks be to God,' I said, 'I thought I'd piss what was in my body.'

I don't remember much more about the night. We said goodbye to the Croftons the following morning and my head splitting with a headache. We headed back for Chicago.

25

I left the Holiday Ballroom one night with the legs unsteady under me and me weary with the world.

'Yes wisha,' I said to myself, 'the devil take you, Mike Daneen. A hall full of women and you didn't move your legs from the counter all night long. Your father gave a long time with the drink before he got sense when he was fifty and took the pledge. Holy Mary, fine girls going by me and saluting me and I couldn't rightly control my two legs. Upon my soul, but this has to stop.'

These were the thoughts that were running through my mind when I was leaving the hall. When I got out on the street I stopped for a while and drew my breath. There were traffic lights directly at the corner of the hall where I had to cross the street to get a bus on the other side that would take me home. While the lights were green I put my hand on the pole to prop myself up. The lights changed and I went across while the traffic was stopped. I tried to walk the white line that was going across the street as if that would help me to walk straight.

'Hey Mike!' someone called. I looked over and back. 'Over here in the car.' I looked over. It was a man from north Kerry that I knew since I came over to Chicago who was talking.

'Come with us in the car,' he said. 'We're going in the direction of your house'. The back door of the car opened.

'Jump in Mike,' he said. 'I think you are a bit on the Kildare side.' I did as he told me and went into the back seat of the car and saluted my friend Pat O'Connor. A woman gave a fine loud laugh from the front of the car. I recognised her immediately.

'Is it you that's there, Jeannie Costello?' I said. She's the girl I took home one night and I had to flee when her father came on the scene. There was another girl sitting beside me in the back seat.

'Mike, I never saw you as heavy from the beer,' said Pat.

'Oh, Pat,' I replied, 'a man without a woman or family is a man that is free.'

I looked at the girl beside me. She was saying nothing but taking everything in. 'And who are you when you're at home?' I said to her, trying to put my hands around her. She turned on me.

'Keep your hands to yourself,' she said, 'because you're all the night drinking.' Then Jeannie spoke from the front seat.

'Kathleen Fitzgerald from Castleisland is her name and you often spoke to her in the Keyman's Club,' she informed me.

Oh my! Drinking and carousing are no good. I made an attempt to fix my two eyes on her and get a right view of her but I wasn't getting on too well. She stayed there and she squeezed into the corner with a foot and a half between us.

'Today is Kathleen's birthday,' Jeannie told me. 'We're going to have tea and some of her cake in her house before we go home. Are you in any hurry, Mike?' she asked me.

I was in no hurry at all. We were driving down Cicero Avenue by this time.

'Look out for Grace Street,' said Kathleen, wiping the fog from the window of the car. Pat turned the car left up a quiet backstreet and parked outside a bungalow with yellow bricks on the front wall. Kathleen jumped out of the car first and the other two followed her. I thought it best to stay where I was for fear I'd get a tongue-lashing. The three of them were walking towards the door. Kathleen looked behind her.

'Where's Mike O'Shea?' she asked, wondering why she hadn't seen me coming. Kathleen ran back to the door of the car and she opened it.

'Yerra, come in for a drop of tea, Mike,' she said. I wasn't feeling too well by this time. 'Come in and don't get pneumonia,' she said.

I followed her in nice and easy. Pat and Jeannie were sitting down at the kitchen table and they giggling like the devil. We all sat at the table while we were waiting for the tea. It wasn't long before the front door of the house opened and a red-haired girl came into the kitchen and who should be with her but my old friend Mike Scollard. Kathleen introduced us to the nice red-haired girl. It was her sister Peig.

'What kind of a meeting is going on here?' Mike said with devilment in his voice. 'Is it a meeting of the bachelors of Kerry?' Then he shouted 'Up Kerry!' To tell the truth, I didn't say anything because I wasn't too comfortable in their company. A cup, a plate and a fork were put in front of each of us. Then Kathleen took a big cake out of the fridge and there were seventeen candles on it. The candles were lit and Kathleen was forced to blow them out.

'What wish did you make?' Mike Scollard asked her. 'I suppose it's a man with a fat bank book you want.'

She said nothing but started cutting the cake. Then Mike Scollard started telling stories.

'I remember the week before I made my first communion,' he began. 'The priest came to the school to examine us. That same morning an old person died in our locality. He lived next to a crossroads. The priest came up to me. "Scollard, who died on the Cross?" was the question he asked me. I answered quickly without thinking. "The Kaiser." That was the name that was on the man who died that morning.'

Pat O'Connor's mouth was full of cake but with the fit of laughing he got, everything in his mouth exploded out all over the table. Kathleen was sitting near me and she was getting great satisfaction from the *craic*. One story leads to another and it was like that with us all night. When somebody looked at the clock it was five in the morning. By that time I had Kathleen well measured. She was a fine, big handsome girl, upon my soul. Why the devil did I drink so much at the dance? It's by mistakes you learn. Suddenly Peig jumped from her chair.

'Have ye any homes to go to?' she demanded.

'We'll go lads, before the red woman upsets the cart,' said Scollard.

When I was going out the front door I noticed Kathleen coming after me. When everybody was talking outside the door, she stuck a piece of paper in my pocket. I didn't let on anything but thanked her and jumped into Pat O'Connor's car. I opened the window to let in some air. She said to me from outside: 'When will I see you again?'

'Yes,' I said to myself in my own mind, 'what's this about?' I told her that I'd ring her during the week.

I went to the twelve o'clock mass the following morning. I can tell you that my head wasn't too healthy. All during mass and I trying to say a prayer, the events of the previous night ran through my mind more than once. It was just as if Satan was there doing his level best to paint those pictures before my eyes. Kathleen Fitzgerald would come before my eyes and I'd see her clearly in her lovely blue dress. Then I'd shake my head.

'Yerra, Mike Daneen, what the devil is wrong with you?' I would say. 'Aren't there a million girls as good as her around the city?'

I'd say another prayer, or I'd try to, but here she'd come again putting something into my pocket. I started searching in my jacket pocket. The left pocket – it wasn't there. The right pocket – it wasn't there. There was no trace of my piece of paper. I thought then that I must have been dreaming or that I had the horrors from the drink. Maybe I never met her. But I must have.

'Oh, God forgive me my sins, isn't it I that have the distraction in the middle of holy mass,' I said to myself.

My sister Máirín had the dinner ready when I reached the apartment.

'What time did you get home this morning?' she asked me, throwing a dirty eye in my direction.

'I can't answer you exactly, but it was brightening for day when I put the key in the door,' I told her. 'Listen,' I said, 'did you find any piece of paper on the floor this morning?' Máirín wasn't too pleased with my antics.

'Was it her that kept you out till morning?' she asked. I answered her sourly.

'Listen here to me now,' I said, 'my mother is in Ireland.' That put her laughing.

'I got the paper,' she told me. 'It's in a mug up in the cupboard.'

Yes, wisha, I wasn't dreaming after all. I ate my dinner and put on the television. But I had no interest in it. Anything that would make noise to take my mind off the beauty of the night before. I couldn't sit still for ten minutes only sitting and rising and walking around the kitchen. I resolved in the end to ring Kathleen. Her phone started ringing.

'Hello,' I said. 'Who am I talking to?' A voice answered.

'Peig here, who's this?' she asked. I told her who I was. I asked her was Kathleen at home. Shortly I heard Kathleen coming to the phone.

'Hello Mike,' she said, 'I thought I had seen the last of you when you left this morning.'

I asked her to go to the dance with me that night. She accepted my invitation on the spot.

It was Johnny O'Connor's band that was playing in the Keyman's that night. I hadn't my leg long over the threshold when Kathleen took my hand and asked me to go out dancing. This was our very first dance together. I can tell you that she was as light as a bird on her feet.

'Where did you learn to dance, Kathleen?' I asked her.

'In a small hall in Scartaglin four miles from Castleisland,' she informed me.

This was one night that I wasn't going to spend hours without moving from the counter. I can tell you that we didn't feel the night going.

We were out dancing the last dance when I got a belt across my shoulders. I looked around and it was Jeannie Costello and Pat O'Connor who were dancing behind us. I saw Jeannie whispering in Kathleen's ear. Then off they went again, Jeannie and Pat. I'm an inquisitive person, at times, and I asked Kathleen what Jeannie had said to her. She was lazy enough at first to give me an answer but after much encouragement she said to me: 'Jeannie was saying that you were a one-night stand,' she said. Don't you know that there's devilment in the minds of some women. But Kathleen said a few words then that will remain in my head forever.

'Understand one thing,' she said, 'I'm not putting you into a corner, if you like you can end it. But if you don't want to, I'll be very happy.' Yes, by God, this girl liked me. 'I know that they're picking on you,' Kathleen said, 'but I'd say that Jeannie is jealous of me.'

'Now Kathleen,' I said, 'tell Jeannie that we have a date next Friday night.'

'And have we?' she asked me.

'Oh we have. And we'll take it one night at a time after that,' I replied. She moved in closer to me. Well, a sensation went through my body like I'd caught a live electric wire. When we were leaving the hall that night, I had half a notion that the disease of love was lying in my bones, yes and in the two of us. Maybe I have enough said now.

I suppose the disease of love takes everyone by surprise. There was no weekend after that when the two of us weren't together. I told her that I wasn't going to spend the rest of my life in America and she told me that she'd be very happy to live in Ireland if that was what I wanted. The two of us started making plans. By the time the two of us had spent ten years in America, we'd be on a good footing as far as money was concerned.

Kathleen Fitzgerald and I got married on 28 April 1962. Because I was playing music all over the city, I knew the world and his mother and they knew me too. On account of that we'd have to have a big wedding, or a very small one with nobody in the church but Kathleen and me and the witnesses. Yes, wisha. We'd have a big wedding.

'Because we'll only be getting married once,' Kathleen said.

Joe Cooley, Seamus Cooley and Mike Keane were the three musicians we hired. But many other musicians were invited. A lot of people were from Castleisland and more were from west Kerry. I can tell you that it wasn't one set that was danced that day but a dozen. At the end of the night all the musicians gathered together in a corner and you couldn't hear finer music anywhere in the world with the various styles blending together.

No week went by that year that I didn't get an invitation to some wedding. We lived in Kathleen's apartment. It was big and cheap and very suitable. Kathleen kept on working in the tea factory and I stayed in Sears Roebuck, not to talk of playing music three nights a week, which left us with plenty of food.

26

In the middle of the year 1962, the manager called me into his office in Sears Roebuck. He asked me would I like to be a Head of Department. I told him that I didn't think I had enough education for those responsibilities, but he told me that I knew every job around me and that was the best certificate I could have. There would be good pay going with the job and a bonus at the end of the year. It's no wonder that I took the job. It took me a while to get used to certain things, but I got great help from the crew who were working with me.

Coming into the end of 1963, there was plenty of work in Chicago for anybody who was looking for it. Things were getting better for the black people too. There were new leaders coming up among them, the likes of Martin Luther King, Jesse Jackson and many more I've forgotten now. It was the Democrats who were in power in the White House in Washington under the leadership of a young, capable man called John Fitzgerald Kennedy. There was a close association between him and Martin Luther King and anybody who read the papers that time could see that Kennedy was doing his best to implement the civil rights Lincoln had guaranteed the black people.

On 22 November 1963, I was sitting in the lunch room in Sears Roebuck and there were a hundred other people there as well. The radio was on as usual and nobody was paying much attention to it. Myself and a man named Bob Rolver were together and we were playing draughts. Suddenly the music stopped and a newsreader came on the air with a news flash.

'President Kennedy was shot while travelling in a motorcade in Dallas, Texas, half an hour ago. An ambulance is taking him to hospital at the moment and he is seriously wounded. We will have more details later.' Nobody in the room said a word, only looking from one to the other in surprise. Even though lunchtime was over, nobody moved but stayed there waiting for further news of Kennedy. Within ten minutes the news came that the president of America had died on his way to hospital with a bullet in his head. There was no more after that and we moved towards our workplace. Out on the floor, a place where people were always running over and back, everybody came almost to a standstill with the fright they got. I never saw people so confused. The president was dead. 'What will we do now?' That's what was on everybody's tongue. I was as upset because of his death as if it was my own brother. I had the privilege of shaking his hand a few years earlier when he was canvassing in Chicago. Now he was dead. When I was walking around, I came upon some black girls. They were crying. One of them said to me,

'What will we do now? He is dead. A man who was doing his best to give our people fair play. Oh, our Abe Lincoln is dead.'

That's they way it was with John F. Kennedy. He will live in the people's memory while they are in this world. A week after his death, everybody was going about their business again and that was for the best.

Apart from the Irish, I think that Kennedy's death affected the black people more than any other group. He had done a lot of work to secure civil rights for them. It is no wonder that Martin Luther King cried on his grave on the day of the funeral. While he was president, he had opened a lot of doors to the black people, but, even though he had improved things, they were still impatient and they wanted to get posts they weren't qualified for. It was mainly the young people who were putting on the pressure for that.

It was in the southern states that the trouble began between the whites and the blacks. The governor of Alabama at that time was George Wallace and, if he had his way, he'd treat the blacks they way Hitler treated the Jews twenty or so years earlier. Martin Luther King was protesting because no black person was allowed to enrol in the State University. George Wallace even stood at the University door with an armed guard and said he'd use them if any black student put their foot across the threshold. Those pictures were shown on every television screen across America.

When the civil rights marches started at first, everything was in order and peacefully organised. But as they went on, the marchers were thinking that their work was having no affect and some of them were getting impatient as a result. There were very few marches but had some trouble following them. The whites were getting afraid that they would be the ones who would suffer from the violence because crowds of blacks might attack white neighbourhoods. In 1966 the riots started in Chicago. Where I was working in Sears Roebuck, it was all blacks who were living in that neighbourhood. Sears Roebuck had to start giving them jobs and soon there were more blacks working there than whites. The summer of 1966 was a hot, sultry summer and we hadn't heat the likes of it for years. Chicago was like every other city at that time because in the poor neighbourhoods there were very few facilities for the youth as regards pastime. There was nothing but apartments built on top of each other without a field or a hall or a sports centre within a couple of miles of them.

These apartments were built as a quick solution to the thousands of people who were coming into the centre of the city looking for accommodation when there was none there for them. They came in from other states and most of them were black. Inside five or six years there was nothing but one big ghetto from Pulaski Road down to Skid Row, the place where all the winos gathered. That district was very close to Lake Michigan. I had to drive through it every day going to and coming from work. There wasn't even a swimming pool in the whole neighbourhood and when the heat came the young people would take the covers off of the fire hydrants. Of course, when the cover was taken off of one of them it would send water up in the air like an oil well and the young people would use the water to cool themselves. It was hard to blame them because they had no other way of doing it and if they went into a swimming pool in a white neighbourhood there would be blue murder.

In the month of July 1966 the black people had a march in every big city. There were riots and murders in some of those cities: Chicago, Brooklyn, Omaha, Baltimore, San Francisco and Jacksonville. The heat in Chicago was between ninety-eight degrees and one hundred and five. With Sears in the middle of the black ghetto, I was looking out for myself because I was a white man. As I said, I had to drive through a black neighbourhood and, because of that, I saw the worst of the troubles.

This particular evening I am talking about, I was driving my Volkswagen north on Homan Avenue and every hydrant on both sides of the street was opened and the water was escaping all over the place. If it happened that there was a fire in any house, there wouldn't be enough water to put it out. Whatever group that was in charge of the water in the city, they turned it all off. Then crowds of young people gathered at every corner. The trouble started at the corner of Madison and Homan. Crowds of young black people started breaking the windows and taking various goods from the shops. The looting was bad enough, but in a short time they set fire to the shops. Police came from every part of the city. A good run is better that a bad stand, I was thinking and I put my foot to the floor of the Volkswagen and headed north as fast as I could. I was never as happy to reach my own house as I was that evening. The way things were looking, a white man had no business in that neighbourhood. I found out from watching the television that night that one black youth was killed and six police were injured. Over three hundred and fifty of the rioters were arrested. Crowds of young blacks went into the white neighbourhoods that were near them and they burned and scorched all before them.

The thing that was bothering me most was how was I going to face into Sears Roebuck the following morning because any white person was in danger of being killed by this time. Kathleen and I were sitting down drinking a sup of tea that evening and we were discussing the state of the city. There were big changes since we first came. There was something wrong when people couldn't go to work without being in danger of being killed. We thought that it would be better for us to map out a different course for ourselves.

When I reached the black neighbourhood the following morning, I slowed down the car to have a look around. I saw an army lorry and twenty soldiers with their guns at the ready near it. Oh thanks be to God, Mayor Daly must have called out the National Guard. I saw soldiers with their guns cocked down the two sides of the street from Madison to Arthington.

No civilians were walking the streets only everybody in cars and they looking suspiciously around them. I suppose people were afraid to put their heads out the door after the devastation of the night before. There was smoke still coming from buildings that were burned to the ground.

That evening, a story appeared on the news that Mayor Daly had met with Martin Luther King and it was a successful meeting. The solution they came to so as to quieten things down was that special caps would be put on the hydrants that would let out some water without putting the whole supply in danger. Then plastic swimming pools would be brought into certain places in the city and they would do until permanent swimming pools were put in their place. Mayor Daly would look for money from the government to build sports centres in the ghettoes.

27

Our first child, a son, was born in 1966 and in the middle of the year 1968, our second child was born, a girl this time. We baptised our son Caoimhín and we called our daughter Deirdre. It was said in folklore that Deirdre was the name of the first pagan queen of Ireland. Both Kathleen and I liked the name very much because it was a fine Irish name.

In and about ninety per cent of the workers in Sears Roebuck were black by this time and if they were under pressure as a people when I went working there first, it's on the white people the pressure was now. I suppose they were looking to get their own back on us. White and black workers were working under me. Some of the black workers said that I favoured the whites and some white workers said that I was a 'nigger lover'. I didn't know was I coming or going. One evening outside the door of Sears Roebuck, two black men came up to me. They asked me was I Mike O'Shea.

'There's one girl working for you,' they said, 'and it would be better for you not to be too hard on her.'

I didn't like that kind of talk at all and I felt that I couldn't put up with this anymore.

As soon as I got home that evening I asked Kathleen to sit down until we had a talk. I told her my story about the warning I got from the two.

'Now Kathleen,' I said, 'life is too short to live in a place where this kind of pressure is coming down on my head.'

We decided there and then that we would go home to Ireland. I'd prefer to live in poverty on the side of the road than to be lying down under anybody.

That night I was talking to my brother Seán on the phone. I told him that I was going back to Ireland as soon as we had things in order.

'Where will you get a job in Carrachán?' he asked me.

'Didn't you hear that they're making a big film back there now?' I replied.

'You're used to making big money,' he said, 'you're used to a car, a television and every other convenience. I make out that you're clean out of your mind if you have it in the head to go home. What about the damp in the houses over there and no heat in them?' I answered him.

'Yerra, I pity your head. There is and heat. Do you remember what our father used to say? "Heat your backside to the turf from Gurrán, you couldn't heat it to better turf." That's natural heat, boy, not the steam heat they have here.'

Seán told me that we'd be back inside a year with every penny spent. Yes, wisha, we'd try it anyway. If we stayed another while in America, Caoimhín would be in school and we wouldn't move at all. Maybe, too, I'd be called up into the army and sent to Vietnam.

Within a month we had everything ready for the road. We sent twenty or so parcels of our clothes and other things home ahead of us in the post. On 19 March 1969, we boarded a plane in O'Hare Airport. Soon she rose into the sky in the direction of Ireland. Kathleen, Caoimhín, Deirdre and I left the big city of Chicago behind us – its troubles and its riches.